942.034

CHILDREN IN RETREAT

An Anthology Of
Evacuee Stories

CHILDREN IN RETREAT

An Anthology Of
Evacuee Stories

Edited By JOY RICHARDSON

SAWD
England

SAWD PUBLICATIONS
Placketts Hole, Bicknor,
Sittingbourne, Kent ME9 8BA.

British Library Cataloguing in Publication Data.
I. Richardson. Joy *1945-*
Children in Retreat: An Anthology of Evacuee Stories.
1. England. Evacuees: Children. Social life,
1936-1945 – Biographies

ISBN: 1-872489-04-4

Printed in Great Britain by Media Print, Sittingbourne, Kent.

Contents

Each child had a label and a small package of personal possessions.   Chatham Evening Post

Introduction

CHILDREN ARE the future. In wartime, this takes on a special significance. Throughout history the famous have made war, leaving the "ordinary" people of a nation to fight it, or endure its consequences.

During the Second World War, Kent was a front-line county. The men and women there had to endure great hardship, the county's children also had to be brave. Because of their proximity, many towns on the capital's outer fringes and London itself were also vulnerable to the relentless enemy air-attacks. In addition, there were the infamous flying bombs, and later, long-range rockets.

The incidence of enemy shelling ranged with regularity through Kent's coastal belt from Margate, Ramsgate and Broadstairs in Thanet; Deal, Dover and Folkestone were also vulnerable areas. On occasions, shelling went further inland at Canterbury and the County Town, Maidstone.

It was against the prospect of heavy casualties that the evacuation of many of the county's children was planned and took place. At the same time an emergency scheme for evacuating London's children also was drawn up. Eighty-three per cent of parents applied for their children to leave. Kent was designated for some (botched up) bureaucratic reason, as a reception area for school children from London.

The preparations for war took root at Government level during the years of appeasement (1936-39). Primitive trenches were dug in

1

London parks, anti-aircraft guns were trundled out (forty-four in all) and warning sirens were tried out over the radio. Regional Commissioners were sent (in secret) to their posts and thirty-eight million gas masks were distributed to regional centres. Fear of gas was an inheritance from the First World War. In the event, no side used gas throughout the years of the second war.

The British ultimatum to the German Government that its troops should leave Poland was delivered at 9 am on 3 September, 1939. It expired at 11 am without a reply. The British people accepted, without complaint, that they were at war with Germany, although contemporary accounts suggest there was surprise at the decision.

Precautions against air attack intensified. Gas masks were issued to the civilian population and (at least for several months) were carried in their cardboard boxes. Street lighting was, by Government decree, extinguished, and car drivers were forbidden to use their headlights. Deaths on the road increased by one hundred per cent.

The most ambitious plan was the evacuation from the supposed danger areas of primary school children and of mothers with children under five. Nationally, four million had been planned for; only one and a half million went, about forty-seven per cent. In addition, two million people made their own private evacuation arrangements.

The Government's evacuation plans were implemented by local authorities. Notices appeared in local newspapers in the danger areas. In the main, these appealed to people's patriotism. King and country apparently expected them to send their children away

Special trains were laid on to take the evacuated children to their destination. Particular memories of that time are of the efficiency of the operation. Trains ran to time, the emergency feeding arrangements worked well, and the real problems only began when the children reached their destination.

Some confusion occurred when, after long journeys, some of the small children reached their destination unlabelled. With luck, some knew their names, but not much more. The "official" labels issued to them when they embarked on their adventures had been lost. Some of the children were ill-equipped to cope with the country conditions in which they found themselves. Over-burdened rural authorities had no funds and for them, even worse, no governmental authority to provide clothing grants. The foster homes in which the children were billeted were often poor themselves. They had no money to provide rubber boots and warm clothing for their visitors.

Billeting evacuee children brought some reward, but not much. The cost each week for each adult was 5/- (25p). The reception family was also given 3/- each week (15p) for each child under fourteen years. This money was paid weekly in advance, at the Post Office. The rates were a little better for the reception of secondary-aged school children. These were 10/6d (50½p) for one child, or 8/6d (40½p) where more than one child was taken. Official logic subscribed to the view that two children could live more cheaply than one. The poor often housed the poor. An official historian recorded... "The wealthier classes evaded their responsibilities throughout the war". Despite war's shadow, the British social structure prevailed.

Since 1938, when war had seemed a real prospect, the problem of the evacuation of the civilian population received constant attention by Government Departments and local authorities who were to be called upon to implement the plans. Few areas of the country had to endure the close and prolonged experience of the evacuation, which, because of its geographical location, had fallen to the lot of Kent. Long range plans emerged in 1938/39, but when the state of emergency had passed, the plans were shelved.

Kent was to be the reception area for 97,000 evacuees from London. Considering its own vulnerability, the logic of this plan was questionable, not simply with the benefit of hindsight. In addition, 39,182 people from the Medway Towns area were to be evacuated to Sittingbourne, Faversham, Whitstable, Herne Bay, Canterbury, Dover, Deal and Sandwich. The main evacuation operation started on 1 September, 1939 (the day Germany invaded Poland) and was completed by 5 September 1939.

There was a constant review of the evacuation areas within the county (see page 43). The course of military events on the continent soon led to an abandonment of the concept that the larger part of the county would be safe. This major flaw apart, there were other more minor ones. A letter from the head teacher of the Hawkinge Council School to the Director of Education for Kent will serve to illustrate the point...

1 April 1939

"Sir,
I feel it is my duty to call the Education Committee's attention to the fact that this school is within eighty yards of the extended aerodrome at Hawkinge and no reasonable parent would allow his or her child to attend a school in what the Air Ministry considers a vital target. . ."

The letter went on to ask that the school be included in the official evacuation plans. By June, 1940, the request was formally granted, and Hawkinge, by virtue of its location, was included as an evacuation area. Other schools were included too. It was realised that they were incapable of offering satisfactory educational facilities. Many teachers were away fighting, schooling was being disrupted by air raids. The educational value of the time being spent by children in school shelters was officially acknowledged. Starting on 19 May, 1940 and finishing on 11 September, 1940, the re-evacuation of children from Kent took place. Their future destinations were many and varied and included Wales, the Midlands, Eastern and Western Counties and Sussex.

Apart from the billeting allowance, the local authorities in the reception areas had no discretion to provide extras for evacuated children. But with Christmas looming, the Good Fairy must have guided the black hand of bureaucracy. The Health Ministry wrote to local authorities to say. . .

"The Minister of Health has allowed for the provision of modest entertainment at Christmas time for evacuated children. The Minister has sanctioned authorities to incur reasonable expenditure (normally 1/- per head) (5p) on such entertainment, at cost to the rates. . ."

There was infinite variety in the official provision of entertainment. The Town Clerk of Blackpool Corporation, writing to the Clerk of the Kent County Council explained how munificent that municipalty had been to Kent's children. . .

"115 children of school age were entertained at parties at various schools, and the children below school age and their mothers attended special treats at the Tower Ballroom, Blackpool. This was a Children's Ballet, followed by a Puppet Show, following which, refreshments were served."

As early as 1940, some evacuees who had been sent away in the earlier tranche from Kent and London, began to drift back. The voluntary nature of the scheme allowed this flow-back to go un-checked. Londoners, who had been billeted in Kent returned home. It had been planned that 136,000 people from London, should go to Kent but only 47,300 arrived. By January, 1940, the number of London's evacuees still in Kent had fallen to 29,653.

By September 1944, the Ministry of Health indicated that evacuees from the evacuation areas in London and Southern England should remain where they were for the time being, but arrangements were put in hand for their return home. The incidence of enemy flying bombs and rockets in November then delayed those plans. Some children did begin to return home and some were with their families for Christmas. The return, unlike the exodus, was gradual. Area by area received back its children.

Thus slowly ended the series of major movements which had taken place under the Government's evacuation scheme. Judged by any standards, it was a stupendous exercise. Since the outbreak of the war in 1939, and during it, forty-eight of Kent's 56 country districts were declared evacuation areas. London apart, no other area in the country said goodbye to so many of its children. Throughout those war years, 67,281 of Kent's children were voluntarily registered to participate in the evacuation scheme.

Many children went away excited by the adventure, too young to recognise the anguish the evacuation caused their parents. Others went away knowing that Father was away fighting (they knew not where) in the war. They were also conscious that Mother remained at home in a situation considered to be too dangerous for them.

With the modern-day pre-occupation with counselling when problems loom, it would be a luxury to speculate on the feelings of both the children, and their families and the subsequent effect evacuation had on their lives. Joan Collins, the actress talking on the BBC's Desert Island Discs Programme to Sue Lawley, during July 1990, summed it up for her. In answer to some probing about her itinerant ways, Joan responded thus ". . .I put it down to my experiences as an evacuee during the war. . .I seemed to be in so many different locations then. . .about six in all. . .Now, I find it difficult to stay put anywhere for long".

The stories in this book are not from mega-stars like Joan Collins, but from people who were prepared to give their personal testimonies of those times. In total, they help to recreate all the humour, trauma and pathos of the Children in Retreat.

The Grass was Greener

by

G.E. FRENCH

WALKING IN Maidstone recently, I saw a coach, full of excited, cheering children just starting off on a European holiday. Clad in light and colourful summer clothing, they were watched by a group of anxious parents all trying to conceal their concern as they waved the coach away to Dover. Beyond was the Channel and the rolling fields and woods of France.

In a moment's reflection, I saw myself nearly fifty years ago. I was a schoolboy then, and I too boarded a coach to leave Maidstone. It was a grey, autumn day, early in the Second World War. The coach was going to London. There was no one to see me off, and I was not sure I had the fare either.

When the war started, I lived with my parents in South-East London. This was in one of the "lost provinces" of old Kent. This Kent stretched to the banks of the Thames at Woolwich and Deptford. It was a place of tightly-packed houses, industry, red buses and clanging London County Council trams. Here and there remained some traces of another time; of rural peace and elegant society, a preserved wood, an old farmhouse, a Georgian mansion, and a church with a spire of timber shingles.

Family talk among the grown ups, and the old folk often centred on the life and times of Kent farm workers, and craftsmen. This was in some far off golden time, before the First World War. Hard old days, but related as good old days. People helped each other, and things were simpler and somehow, less fussed. Nobody had any money, of course, but what you had went a long way. The grass was greener, the sun was brighter and in the winter the snow lay deep, crisp and even. There were roast chestnuts and ale mulled with a red hot poker. Kent sounded so good!

I took it all in, as I walked the sad, suburban streets amidst the screeching trams, and smelly lorries. I vowed that I would one day go and see for myself. I would be a Kent Cob, and wander in sunlit, glorious freedom among the leaves so green-O!

It happened sooner than I bargained for. The "phoney" war had been on for quite some time with absolutely nothing happening. Suddenly things changed. It all began to look rather nasty. The Government decided that the children left in this vulnerable area should be dispersed to a place of safety. It was 1940, I was 13 years old. My school was to go to Eccles, a village near Maidstone. Before long, we found ourselves boarding a train. Each boy and girl was equipped with a suitcase, a gas mask, a packet of sandwiches and an apple. Firmly tied to our coat lapels was a cardboard label, with our names and destination. In each pocket was a stamped and addressed postcard to inform our mothers that we had arrived safely. The departure was somewhat fraught. There were red-eyed mothers trying desperately to stiffen the upper lip, and to smile encouragement at the same time. The children, for the most part, were wild with excitement. The boys, in particular, were under the erroneous impression that they were getting rid of grown ups for ever.

Our arrival at our destination was something of a disappointment. We were met by quite kind, if slightly desperate ladies, who took us to our billets in Victoria Road. These turned out to be rows of yellow brick, terrace houses, with slate roofs. They looked exactly the same as the grim rows of Victorian barracks that we knew in Lewisham and Lee Green. There were no roses around the door, and no birds

8

nesting in thatched eaves. Was this really the country? In the distance though, we could see the lift of the chalky downs and a river flashed in the sunlight. Nearby, there were orchards and woods. Perhaps it wouldn't be too bad after all.

The village had been built, we were told, by a paper making company. Most of the people living there were still paper makers. They worked hard, lived quietly and went to bed early. It was expected that we would do the same. Tomorrow we could attend the village school. Meanwhile, we should occupy ourselves usefully, and quietly.

The school had been built by the Church of England, a century before, for a tiny rural population. It was now suddenly required to deal with a regiment of somewhat bewildered and alien children, all of highly differing abilities and temperaments. The staff were mainly elderly women. The school simply collapsed under the strain. So did some of the women. Eventually, we were told to attend on alternate mornings only. For the rest of the time, we were to try to make ourselves useful and to keep out of mischief. We tried, but it was a situation ripe with the seeds of inevitable juvenile disaster.

For a while, we helped to dig slit trenches in the recreation ground. We listened attentively to lectures given by grizzled ex-army N.C.O.'s about what to do in a gas attack and how to give the alarm if parachutists were seen. There were dire warnings about something called the "fifth column", and the necessity of being alert to strange people on bikes at night doing odd things with torches. The significance of this was lost on us!

We walked about for some time. Our heads were permanently bent backwards as we scanned the skies for the enemy hordes descending. This got rather painful, and we rather lost interest, particularly when we were refused permission to arm ourselves with pitchforks. We took to following perfectly innocent housewives cycling home in the evening dusk. We thought they might be members of the "fifth column", whatever that was? But authority rapidly·stopped that. There seemed to be nothing we could usefully do, except explore the countryside. This we set off to do, in the best traditions of David Livingstone and Robinson Crusoe.

A small group of us, provisioned with a bottle of "Tizer" and a bag of licorice allsorts, set off one morning with a vague idea of somehow reaching the distant river. We soon left the lanes and walked through a gap in the hedge into the green aisles of a hop garden. Then on into a large orchard. As we walked, we decked ourselves with garlands of hops, and ate the sweet and juicy pippins, which we picked from the laden boughs. We found a hay-rick, and tumbled and roared about in the soft, yielding, sweet-smelling hay. This was more like it! This must be what being in the country was all about! In a field nearby, a flock of sheep stared warily at us. We advanced to stroke them, but they seemed unaccountably alarmed, and ran away. We gave chase, whooping like Red Indians, but could not catch them. It all seemed good fun, and we hoped they had enjoyed it too. All the same, there seemed to be rather a lot of bleating and baaing.

Suddenly, we saw a man in shirt sleeves and braces running towards us over the fields. His face was very red and he seemed greatly agitated. He was shouting and shaking his fist. From his thunderous expression, we gathered he was not pleased. The situation seemed full of menace, and we unanimously decided on a rapid retreat – at speed. It all seemed a bit peculiar since we had been told that you could do what you liked in the country. Folk were reputed to be friendlier than those back home.

Somewhat subdued, but still eager to explore, we found our way into a deep, chalky cutting in the woods. This led us into a huge disused quarry, rather like a Kentish Grand Canyon. There were railway lines with old trucks standing about. There were tumbledown signals and lever points. These shifted the rusty rails with screeches and groans. Soon we were operating our own private little railway. There were boys in the trucks, boys pushing and boys operating the levers and points. It was all great fun, but the proceedings eventually came to a halt. Some points, when shifted made the line terminate in a large pool of deep green water which lay in one corner of the quarry. The truck only went in half way, but we couldn't get it out. We all got wet, particularly the boy who stepped into a large hole in the bottom of the pond.

It had been quite an eventful day. We trudged home, quite happily, though somewhat the worse for wear. Most of us had bramble rips, sodden shorts and shirts. They got a bit upset back at the billet because of the trail of chalky wet footprints on the polished lino.

A few days later a policeman visited the school. The aged headmistress told the whole school, that grave complaints had been made. Our sins were listed as trespass, vandalism and petty larceny. We were not quite sure what petty larceny was, but it sounded quite bad. Enquiries were being made, she said. When the culprits were discovered, they would be severely dealt with by the magistrates. We were dismayed. Life in the country was definitely not as we had been led to believe. What would happen if we were discovered? Did they still send people to Botany Bay?

Later that week, masses of German aeroplanes droned high overhead, like silver fish in the deep blue of the Kentish skies. At night all hell broke loose. Jettisoned bombs screeched down to explode in the woods and fields. Shrapnel and spent bullets pattered on the slate roofs, like hail. Shattered aeroplanes plummeted down, and crashed in great spouts of smoke and flame. Night after night, we were dragged from warm beds and shoved into the cupboard under the stairs, with buckets of sand, water and a stirrup pump. This really was not at all like the Shangri La the old people at home had talked about. First, there was the threat (real to us) of Botany Bay. Now, the Germans were trying to get us. I decided, enough was enough. I had been away for four months, but it had felt like a life-time.

The next morning, I wrote a note for the good people who had been lumbered with a strange evacuee kid from London. I packed my bag, and walked into Maidstone. At the bus depot, I saw a "Green Line" coach with "London" on the front. I climbed onboard and sat down. When the conductor came round to collect the fares, we were well past Wrotham. I was sixpence short of the fare. I told the conductor my tale, and he agreed to take my name and address for the missing sixpence (it was never requested).

I arrived home just after dark. My mother answered the door bell, and stared at me with a mixture of astonishment and alarm. "I've come home" I announced, unnecessarily . . . "And before you start, I can tell you now, its not free-er and nicer in the country like you said." "There's no peace and quiet either."

*In spite of his first introduction to the Kent countryside, **Geoff French** returned to the county to live following his retirement. Mr. French now lives in Maidstone after a career as a quantity surveyor much of which was spent abroad in Africa. He is married but has no children.*

11

Flight On The Golden Eagle
by
CHRISTINE GARDNER

DURING THE days leading up to the beginning of World War Two, there were various meetings and arrangements going on in Gravesend and the surrounding areas. All were intended to prepare us for the event of war. We had already been fitted with gas masks. These ranged from the "Mickey Mouse" look for toddlers, all-encasing ones for tiny babies, to the ordinary standard black type for older children and adults. When first putting them on, they had an awful suffocating effect, but after much perseverance and determination not to panic, they could be tolerated. From time to time we had to return to an allocation centre for small modifications to be made to counteract the different types of gas the masks might have to endure. Fortunately, as it turned out, we were all in the happy position of never ever having to use them. Nevertheless, from the very first day of the war, these gas masks were to accompany us wherever we went.

The most important preparation was the evacuation of children from areas the Government considered vulnerable to enemy bombings. As

Gravesend was situated on the edge of the River Thames, and only a few miles from London, it was considered a high risk area.

Gravesend Borough Council embarked on what was an extremely efficient and successful operation to get children, and some parents, evacuated to a place of safety. Schools were contacted, registers were set up with names of parents who wished their children to be evacuated. Meetings were arranged to ensure everyone knew exactly what was happening, and the following notices appeared in the Gravesend Reporter: (See facing page).

Another notice read:

"Every effort will be made in the reception areas to make children and others as happy as possible in their new homes. The exact areas where the local evacuated persons will be housed cannot be disclosed officially but we have reason to believe that the plans are for reception in the rural areas of Norfolk and Suffolk.

The Northfleet and Gravesend children will sail from Southern Railway Pier. Times of sailings have been notified to all parents and also the points at which they should assemble. Loud speakers have toured the streets of Gravesend telling parents children should attend their schools to receive instructions with regard to evacuation plans. Enough food should be taken for 24 hours".

So it was that my brother, my sister and myself, all pupils of Northcourt School, Gravesend, along with many other children, assembled at the school at 6 am on Sunday, 3rd September 1939, to be evacuated to a place of safety. We were all tremendously excited. We thought we were going on a lovely holiday. We were of such tender years that we could not envisage what such a separation from our homes and parents would be like.

We arrived at school, each child with a haversack on his/her back. Our parents had been advised to supply us with a haversack rather than a suitcase or bag, as this would leave our hands free. My mother had made one for each of us from a type of black oil skin (similar in appearance to PVC). Each one contained the articles we were officially instructed to take pyjamas, slippers, a change of underwear, toilet requisites (including tooth-brush and tooth-paste). How grown up I felt. For the first time in my life, I had been allowed to have a whole block of Gibbs toothpaste entirely to myself, instead of having to share with my brother and sister! We also had to take enough food for twenty four hours.

14

Fletcher, Mayor.

BOROUGH OF GRAVESEND.

NOTICE

THE British Empire and its trusted Allies, France and Poland, are at War with Germany.

Our beloved King and our Prime Minister have addressed to you messages calling for calmness and resolution and to these messages it is not for me to add.

I wish, however, to say that I am confident that the people of Gravesend will, as in 1914-1918, do their duty in the trying times that doubtless lie before them. We have to face a ruthless and determined enemy and one who will shrink from no deceit, treachery or atrocity in order to achieve his ends. Do not let us under-rate him, but resolve to meet him with inflexible fortitude and loyalty to His Majesty The King.

May the Almighty Succour and Bless you all.

WALTER C. FLETCHER,
Mayor.

GOD SAVE THE KING

After a few formalities, we set forth with our haversacks on our backs and our gas masks to the front of us. Each child had identifying labels tied to his/her coat and luggage. We kissed our parents goodbye. We were unable to comprehend that we wouldn't be seeing them again for a while. What utter heart-ache our parents must have felt, torn between sending us to a place of safety, or keeping us with them. Some parents did accompany their children, but the vast majority of children went on their own. We proceeded from Northcourt School, to the Southern Railway Pier at West Street Station, accompanied by some of the teachers from our school. On arrival, we filed along the platform, across the bridge and onto the jetty, where we could see children and parents already embarked aboard the 'Royal Daffodil'. After a while, we watched it pull away, and its place was taken by the paddle steamer 'Golden Eagle'. We walked up the gangway of the waiting vessel and found ourselves a seat close to the guard-rail. I was very happy that we had been able to find a seat to accommodate my brother Raymond, my sister Betty, my friend Maisie and myself. My mother had instructed my brother, who was the eldest, to look after us. But along with all the other boys, he was carried away in his imagination; he thought himself a 'Captain' of this wonderful ship. He was about to embark on a swashbuckling adventure! Scattered around the deck were boxes of apples for us to help ourselves, and we had been supplied with plenty of sweets. The boys at once started to explore; the girls sat very close together on the wooden slatted seats, taking in the scene around us, and wondering about the future. We did not feel unduly sad or anxious at the time, because we felt we were going on holiday. We were all very eager to get on with it! Eventually, we became aware of a rumbling which seemed to come from the bowels of the ship, and to our great excitement, we saw the paddle wheels begin to turn. We moved gently away from the jetty, pulled out into the middle of the river, and started our journey downstream. Everyone on board cheered and waved to parents, friends and the Mayor of Gravesend, Councillor Walter C. Fletcher and Members of the Corporation, who had come to see us off. Our eyes searched the shore for places that were familiar to us: St. George's Church, where I had been christened, West Street Pier, where the car ferry then operated between Gravesend and Tilbury. The present day passenger ferry now runs from West Street, the Town Pier, now no longer in use, the Royal Terrace Pier and Gravesend Promenade. At the back of the promenade, we could just see Fort Gardens, which houses an early fort, built to repel enemy ships from coming up the river.

Three thousand six hundred and ninety four persons were evacuated from Gravesend in three hours that day. Everything went off perfectly thanks to all the helpers and marshalls who controlled the operations, and the Town Clerk and his staff, who did a magnificent job prior to, and including the evacuation.

There were five vessels in all transporting evacuees from Gravesend to East Anglia: 'Royal Daffodil', 'Golden Eagle', 'Royal Sovereign', 'Medway Queen' and 'Queen of the Channel', three of which were paddle steamers. Little did we know that in the not too distant future, some of these ships would again feature in an 'evacuation' – the evacuation of our retreating soldiers from Dunkirk (one of whom would be my father).

The weather was beautiful as we continued to make our way down the river. When we reached the estuary, the paddle steamer began to slow down, and finally came to a halt. The weather was by this time rapidly deteriorating. All sorts of suggestions were made by the boys for the reason for stopping – not least was that we were in close proximity to a German U boat and had to turn off our engines and remain silent! In fact, it was because we were to be joined at Southend by British warships, who were to escort us to our destination. We were not aware of this at the time, and although we must have been hugging the coast line, we did not see land again until we reached Great Yarmouth. War had been declared, and announced on the wireless whilst we were en route, but it was thought prudent not to reveal this to us.

During the journey on the boat, I plucked up courage to go below to where we were told some drinks would be served. I tottered and swayed my way down and got my drink. I was just returning, when the boat gave a sudden lurch, and down I went, drink and all. I landed full square on my bottom. I can still rember the pain; it really hurt! After having a few tears, I picked myself up, minus my drink, and went back on deck. With the resilience of a youngster, I put it to the back of my mind, but the incident has stayed in my memory ever since.

Another incident was when one of the girls accidentally dropped her purse over the rail and lodged itself close to the paddle wheel.

She was rather upset about this, and a member of the crew climbed over the rail (amid claps and cheers from us all) to retrieve the purse. He was a hero in our eyes.

It was now late afternoon, and because the boat had been pitching slightly, I was beginning to feel a bit queasy. All round me, children and parents had succumbed to sea sickness. I was lucky to have lasted thus far. It may have been due to the barley sugar sweets my Mum had insisted on giving us as we left home that morning. She impressed upon us that if we sucked one from time to time during the boat journey, we would be less likely to be sea sick. I think by now though, the stabilising effect was beginning to wear off. Just as I was wondering how I was going to cope, the motion of the vessel changed and I realised we were slowing down and approaching land. Sea sickness was forgotten like magic, and everyone started laughing and chatting as we pulled alongside the landing. For a while we became engrossed in watching the docking procedure. Eventually the gangways were in place and ready for us to leave. After being counted and instructed to stay close to our teachers, we gathered up our belongings and disembarked two by two, just like the animals from the Ark. No doubt we were just as bewildered! Because we had been afloat for a long time, as we stepped ashore, our legs felt very wobbly. For a while, we needed all our concentration to put one foot in front of the other to walk straight. However, with each step, our balance improved, but we were all very glad to be once again on terra firma.

The romance we started with the paddle steamer 'Golden Eagle' that sunny morning had come to an end. I know I speak for others when I say, it was a romance we have never forgotten. Whenever mention is made of the 'Golden Eagle' our thoughts immediately go back to that exceptional journey on the 3rd September, 1939.

After vacating the ship, we did not have far to go before we came to a large old red brick school. Here we were to spend the night. After being fed, we made our way to a large upstairs room, which may have been the school hall or gymnasium. We were given large sacks full of straw, one to each child. These were to be our beds for the night. They were surprisingly comfortable. When the time came to settle down we were allowed to go in small groups to the wash rooms to clean our teeth. This was the first time I had occasion to use 'my own' toothpaste. It felt great! We were told to try to get to sleep quickly as we had another journey ahead of us the next day. We still had no idea where we were going, and we were too young to think of asking. As for going straight to sleep, it was almost impossible. Many of the boys were still in high spirits. Occasionally, someone's slipper or shoe would come flying through the air, closely followed by a body trying to retrieve the lost article. Eventually, peace did descend.

It was at this point, trying to sleep, that I realised this was not just a holiday. I felt sad and very homesick. I had been away from home before, when I was five and had had to spend a short time in hospital. I had always accepted these things. Now, in the darkness, a sense of foreboding came over me and I felt absolutely lost, lonely and unhappy. I just wanted to go back home to my mother. I was nine years old and should not give way to tears, but in the darkness, nobody could see me! I wondered how many more of those children felt as I did. Throughout the whole of that day and evening my brother, my sister and all the other children with us had maintained a stoic manner. It was a conscious effort, born of necessity, which we sensed was expected of us.

I eventually drifted off to sleep, but this was to be short lived. In the early hours of the morning – it was still totally dark – we were all awakened by the sound of the air raid siren, which must have been located just outside the window. The sound of the siren wailing was frightening. It unsettled us all. But it was not long before we heard the 'all-clear'. Great Yarmouth it appeared had not been affected by the raid that night.

Morning came, and with the daylight some of my fears subsided. We washed, dressed and breakfasted on sausages. I remember the huge pans they brought round from which we helped ourselves to a sausage to go with the bread we had been given. The conversation during breakfast was all about our very first air raid.

After breakfast it was time to continue our journey. Loading our haversacks once more onto our backs, and not forgetting our gas masks, we accompanied our teachers to where coaches were waiting to take us to the surrounding towns and villages. We were given a brown carrier bag which contained various items of food. These were, the largest bar of chocolate I had ever seen, a tin of corned beef, some biscuits, a tin of milk and one or two other items. These were intended for the person with whom we would be staying.

As the coaches gradually filled with children, the teacher in charge ushered herself and about eight of us onto one of the coaches. After travelling for some time, we pulled up outside a large building. We clambered out onto the pavement with all the other children and we were instructed to wait whilst the teacher made enquiries as to where we should go. She quickly returned and informed us that we had boarded the wrong coach and were not in the area designated for our particular school. We returned to the coach and went on our way to the correct area. This was Toftwood, a suburb of the country town of East Dereham, about thirty-five miles from Great Yarmouth.

At Toftwood village school, we were pleased to see some of our fellow pupils. By this time it was obvious that a great many of them had gone to homes in the village. Only a handful were left. This included my brother, my sister, my friend Maisie and myself. We must have looked a sorry sight. Our home-made haversacks were beginning to deterioriate. What with the wear and tear when hoisting them onto our shoulders and the rough treatment they had received from some boisterous boys during our overnight stay at Great Yarmouth, it was little wonder they were ready to collapse.

Whilst drinking a glass of milk, given to us as we entered the school, we became aware that a plump bespectacled lady in a spotted white dress was taking an interest in us. When she heard that Maisie and I were friends, she said she would take us both. My brother and sister were about the last to be accommodated. The person who took them really only wanted one evacuee, but my brother said he could not leave my small sister. She relented, and took them both.

Maisie and I accompanied our lady up the little village street until we came to a bungalow set in a long front garden. When we entered, I remember seeing a shy, young man sitting at a table which had been prepared for tea. He had a newspaper held up in front of him. The lady told us that her name was Mrs. Smith and the young man behind the newspaper was her brother, George. When introduced, George quickly popped his head round the edge of the paper, said "Hello" and then went back to his reading. When he had relaxed a little over tea, we began to chat to one another. George was a young man in his late twenties and he and his sister were very much alike in appearance. Both had very dark hair, ruddy complexions and wore spectacles. Later, another gentleman came in and introduced himself as Mr. Smith. He had light brown curly hair, a big broad smile, and a kind face. The last one to make our acquaintance was a little black and white mongrel dog named 'Whisky'. This was especially nice for me, as I had had to say goodbye the previous day to our beloved pet dog, 'Topsy'.

After tea, we wrote a short note to our respective parents, and Mrs. Smith completed an official post card with her name and address, which was also sent to our parents. (The authorities had thought of everything)! Whilst we were doing this, a knock came to the side door. I was delighted when I saw my brother and sister, in the company of a lady, named Mrs. Hall. She had come to inform us that my brother and sister would be staying with her and her family who lived just down the road. Eventually, it was time for Maisie and I to go to bed, and we went happily to sleep (both in one double bed). We were too tired to dwell on our family partings. Mr. and Mrs. Smith, and George treated us in a quiet, gentle and friendly manner, and so we did not feel at all overwhelmed.

For a while, the evacuee children joined the village children at their school. The building was very old and small – two or three rooms. One was partitioned off to make more room for us. Each room had an open fireplace, and if it was too cold for us to go out to play in the playground, we would gather around the fire. This was protected by a huge fire guard. Here we drank our milk allocation, which we had every day. Because of the large number of children attending the small school, it was considered unsuitable for adequate teaching. It was decided that half the children would attend morning school, and the other half in the afternoons. As far as we were concerned, this was a lovely idea, but maybe the teachers held different views. On the half days when evacuees were not at the village school, we had to assemble at the Gospel Hall building, a few yards down the road. We were supervised by our own teachers and we would read books, tell stories, act plays or go on nature rambles. To compensate for this, we had homework in the three R's, which *had* to be done. George used to help Maisie and I with our 'arithmetic' homework. One day we had a particularly nasty 'long division'. With George's help, we had the right answer. The next day at school we were told to stand up as we were the only two in the class with the correct answer. I cannot recall whether our consciences caused us embarrassment, nor whether the teacher realised how we had both come to have the same answer!

During September 1939, the Mayor of Gravesend, Councillor Walter C. Fletcher, came to Norfolk to visit the evacuees to see how we were settling in. He reported back that we were 'all happy'.

Another rather nice gesture was the competition set up by Mr. Barnes of the Rainbow Stores, Gravesend, offering ten shillings (50p) for the best essay each week from a boy and girl evacuee. There were painting and crossword competitions. One I remember was 'What I Miss Most'. I entered, and my reply, along with many others, was printed in the 'Gravesend Reporter'. What I missed most was going out with my Dad in the car on Sundays. The newspaper printed each week a page of letters written by evacuees. One girl won one of the competitions devised by Mr. Barnes, and the prize was a bicycle. She returned to Gravesend to be presented with the cycle and when she came back to Toftwood, she was the envy of everyone.

In November 1939, the Borough Council organised a coach trip for any parent who wished to visit their child.

Unfortunately, my parents were unable to take advantage of this offer, but Maisie's father came. He brought us all gifts from home, and it was lovely to see him.

My brother, sister and I were delighted a few weeks later when my father managed to get a few days leave from his unit in France. Despite the snow and cold weather, he and my mother paid us a surprise visit. They stayed for a few days. We just walked, talked and enjoyed one another's company. It was so hard to say goodbye.

The days immediately leading up to Christmas were very cold, but we wanted to go carol singing. I think our mothers, had they known, would have been rather apprehensive, but we had, by then, learned that village life was quite different from our own town life. Mrs. Smith said we could go. She had warned some of the neighbours in advance that we would be calling.

Our first 'victim' was our immediate neighbour, a dear old gentleman by the name of Mr. Lilly. He endeared himself to us whenever we met him by showing us a particularly fine gold pocket watch, of which he was very proud. It was attached to a gold chain which he wore across the front of his waistcoat, and the magnificent watch fitted nicely into his pocket. He would open the back and show us all the wonderful workings. He also carried with him a bag of fruit bon-bon sweets, each individually wrapped and with a picture on the front of the fruit it contained. If we were lucky, he would offer us one.

After calling on Mr. Lilly, we continued on down the road and sang a carol at each bungalow, and everyone seemed very pleased. Most of the bungalows had long drives, and the walking and singing was wearying. Our return home was abruptly decided for us when we called at the next home, the occupants of which had not been informed by Mrs. Smith that her two evacuees would be carol singing that evening. We were well in the throes of 'Away in a Manger', when a deep voice boomed out "Clear off or I'll throw a bucket of water over you". Needless to say, we did not wait to explain who we were, but ran full pelt down the drive and back home as fast as we could. It must have dampened my enthusiasm for carol singing ever again, because that was the first and last time I ever attempted it. The next day we received an apology, via Mrs. Smith, from the embarrassed neighbour.

Christmas morning arrived and Maisie and I awoke early. We were so excited at the prospect of having our Christmas presents. Although it was still dark, we got out of bed and started to unwrap the packages, which had been placed at the foot of the bed. I think guilt must have intervened because we decided to re-wrap all the parcels and start afresh in the morning. When daylight came, it was wonderful! I had been given a most magnificent primrose yellow tea set. Maisie had a blackboard and easel. There were various gifts, including a doll each, books and sweets. But I think our favourite item was a small brown handbag each. The all important thing was that each bag contained our very first make-up. There was a small powder compact (I remember mine was silver with big bright stones on the lid, the like of which would only be found today in an antiques shop). There was also a box of real face powder to put in the compact, and a tiny box of rouge. But, I don't recall any lipstick! Tucked into a little side pocket was a mirror and a purse. How grown up we both felt! We treasured those handbags.

The Smith family were very kind to us, and gave us as good a Christmas as they could possibly manage. Looking back, I hope we brought something a little special to their Christmas. They had no children of their own. We later went with them to their relatives, and joined in their festive fun.

On the 27th December 1939, all the evacuees from Toftwood and surrounding areas were invited to a Christmas party at the Assembly

Rooms in East Dereham. During the evening we were told that "when we grew older, we would realise that we had, by being evacuees, done something to help the great national effort".

The place was decorated with coloured lights and streamers. We sat down to a lovely tea. This was followed by some good entertainment. The conjuror was the highlight for me. He was the Vicar of East Dereham, the Reverend L.E. Baumer. He held us all spellbound with his varied tricks. This included the white rabbit from the top hat, but the ultimate for me was when he produced real sweets from a hollow metal tube and then threw them to us to eat. I couldn't believe he had actually made sweets from nothing! We went home that evening very happy children.

The winter of 1939/40 proved to be a very hard one. To children who had come from the mild south east, the chilly east coast was a new experience. It just snowed and snowed. When it eventually stopped, the snow ploughs came through the village pushing the snow into great mountains on each side of the road which, for children is exciting. But we found the bitter cold winds hard to cope with. I can remember my brother pulling a sledge along the road. His knees were black and blue with cold. He had a warm muffler around his neck, but his knees were completely bare. Then, long trousers were worn only by men and teenagers.

The people of Norfolk did not seem to mind the cold. As soon as the ponds and lakes froze over, out came the ice skates. It was wonderful to see them skating with such expertise. My sister and I were once invited by Mrs. Hatfield (the lady who owned the village shop), to go skating with her to a place near East Dereham known locally as 'The Nettard'. She was a competent skater. We got no further than just sliding around the ice.

During the hard winter, the pond at the bottom of the road, just beside, the school, froze up. For weeks it had had thick ice on it, and was perfectly safe to walk on. On this particular day, a large group of us, including Maisie and my brother, were playing around on the ice. Maisie found a piece of an old bicycle pedal and, for the want of something better to do, she started to wind it round and round on the cold surface. The next moment we heard a loud crack as the ice gave away. Everyone scattered, but I found myself with one leg completely submerged in water. My brother quickly grabbed me and pulled me out. My thick black woollen stockings were saturated. I thought Mrs. Smith would be cross with me, and so was afraid to go back to the house. My brother, thinking he was doing the right thing, walked me round until my stockings were almost dry. When I did eventually get home, George was the only one in. Realising how upset I felt, he quickly organised the drying of my stockings. Nobody was any the wiser.

A few days later my knees swelled up, and I became quite crippled for a time. For my sins, when my mother heard how poorly I was, she decided I should have a course of Sanatogen to help me recover. It tasted absolutely vile. The only way I could manage to take it was if I stood at the open back door, pinched my nose, and downed the stuff in one gulp. It was like drinking thick white plaster. Eventually, Mrs. Smith realised my plight, and called a halt to my medication.

With the ease and speed unique to children, we became integrated into the life of the village. We attended the local Sunday school. This was held in a little wooden church. Miss Dines was our teacher, and each week she would give us a lovely picture text. We wandered the fields and fens to our hearts' content, but we were always warned of the unpredictable marshland fens. One could find oneself rapidly sinking in certain areas.

One autumn afternoon, we decided to walk across the waterlogged fields. We came to a barred gate, but to pass through the gate to get to the road, we had to squelch through the thickest mud. The mud came up and over the tops of our 'wellies'. In the end, we had to abandon them and go barefoot. When we got back to the road, we found a clear puddle in which to clean our feet. Had we been more experienced in the ways of the 'country' we would not have even attempted to cross the muddy fields at that time of the year. However, we soon learned the do's and don'ts of the rural scene.

We made friends with the village children. We soon discovered that Barney Walpole was a real character. His parents grazed and tethered their goats on the meadow which ran beside the main village road. Most days, Barney could be found sitting on a gate, carefully peeling a turnip or swede which he then ate with great relish. He would also, very impishly, threaten us, and any other unsuspecting wanderers as they walked through the meadow with the family goats. Some of these had large horns. He was also known for chasing all the girls and attempting to kiss them, which of course, brought squeals of panic from us whenever he came into sight.

25

Maisie and I were extremely fortunate to have been befriended by one of our teachers who came with us from Gravesend – Miss Evans. She was a very likeable Welsh lady. From time to time, she would invite us to have tea with her at the home of the people with whom she was billeted. They were Mr. and Mrs. Rallison. They did all they could to make us feel at home in Toftwood. At Christmas time, we were asked to tea with them. To our delight, in the centre of the tea table was a 'snow slide with snowballs', all beautifully made from cotton wool. It was lovely. But there was more! After we had finished eating, Mrs. Rallison rolled a snowball down the slide to each of us. Each one contained a small gift. We spent a very happy evening with them. Just before it was time to go Mr. Rallison said, "If you come to the front door I think you will find Father Christmas has been". Excited, we went to look. There, on the front door mat, lay several parcels. That charming couple had gone to the trouble of wrapping a Christmas gift for each of us. I have never forgotten the happy times we spent there.

Saturday afternoon, rain or shine, we would all walk into East Dereham to go to the local cinema, stopping first at the village shop to buy a pennyworth of sweets. What a treat this was. In Gravesend we had never been to a cinema.

When we arrived, we joined all the other children pushing and jostling their way to the box office, where we handed over our entrance fee of two (old) pennies. When we got inside, it was complete bedlam for a while. But as soon as the lights went down and the film started, everyone became engrossed. During the interval we all had a good sing-song, including 'Roll out the Barrel'.

When it was all over, we would make our way slowly back home to tea; still living in the land of make-believe, and taking on the role of the characters we had just seen in the films.

Our journey home was varied. We had to cross the railway at a level crossing just outside East Dereham. A child could spend hours just watching the gates open and close each time a train was due. In those days, the trains were hauled by steam locomotives and each time one passed, the engine driver would wave to us from the footplate. There was an exciting atmosphere about the place.

Sometimes we would amble the other way home, and explore St. Nicholas' church and the churchyard at East Dereham. The fascination for us there was St. Withburga's Well. This was a well or spring in a sunken garden, completely enclosed by an iron fence. There was a plaque bearing details of the sainted Withburga. She was the daughter of the seventh century King Anna of East Anglia, and she lived a very pious life. Upon her death she was buried in the churchyard, but in the tenth century the Abbot and monks of Ely stole her body and placed it in Ely Cathedral. From then on, a spring of water appeared where her body had lain for 300 years.

Continuing on from the churchyard, we had to go through a large meadow, which more often than not contained grazing cows. I did not like them, but my fear would be forgotten when we began to play 'jump the cow pat'. We devised a game to see how many we could jump over, and who would be the first to land in one! When we reached the village, if we had time, it would be once round the meadow to tease Barney's goats, then off home to tea.

Sometimes, on a Saturday afternoon, or Sunday morning, Mrs. Smith would ask us to go to a nearby market garden, which was situated at the end of the village, bordered by open countryside. There were several greenhouses and we would have to walk through them until we found someone to serve us. More often than not, we would be served with a cucumber picked straight from the plant. They were absolutely delicious. On most days our tea consisted of cucumber sandwiches, followed by two chocolate tea cakes.

Next to the market garden, we discovered some pigs. At first we were a little nervous of them, but as our visits became more frequent, we would climb onto the walls of their styes so that we could stroke them. They appeared to like this because they would stand on their hind legs and nuzzle us. They were beautifully clean and pink. When they had their babies, it was a double delight – all those squeals and little curly tails! If we were lucky, our visits would coincide with feeding time, which was a real free-for-all. The pungent smell of their food did not deter us one bit.

During my stay in Toftwood, I was lucky and spent the entire time at one home. My brother and sister were not so fortunate. Mrs. Hall, the lady with whom they were happily billeted, began to suffer ill health, so they had to be found new homes. My brother was found accommodation with Mrs. Bolton and her son Fred. He was very happy there, and got on well with them. Mrs. Bolton was the first lady I had ever seen riding a motor-cycle. She was an extremely kind person.

Whilst we were staying in Toftwood, she had occasion to travel to Kent. She went out of her way to call upon my mother to give her news of us. On another occasion, my brother Raymond accompanied her on her motorcycle when she had to go to Kent, and visited my mother for a few hours.

My sister's new home turned out to be a disaster. The people were very unkind to her. It was probably as a result of her continual unhappiness that my mother decided we should return to Gravesend. My friend, Maisie, had already returned home just after Easter 1940. Also, the bombing raids on Norwich were beginning to be heard at Toftwood. All this, plus the fact that the Gravesend authorities were starting to compile a register of the names of children whose parents wished them to take part in a second evacuation, brought about our return to Gravesend in May 1940. Seventy-four children had been evacuated from Northcourt School to Norfolk. We must have been the last to return.

It was sad to say 'goodbye' to Mrs. Smith. This was a lady whom I had called 'Mum' for nearly ten months. It is a long time in a child's life. We had become part of the close-knit country life. We had also cultivated the wonderful Norfolk dialect, so much so, that I'm sure we truly fitted the description of 'Norfolk Dumplings'.

Christine Gardner now lives in Deal near Dover in Kent. She is married with a grown up family and works on a voluntary basis in a charity shop for the Children's Society.

Down the Primrose Path

by

CHRISTINE GARDNER

WE HAD only been home from Norfolk for a few weeks when we were plunged into preparations for our second evacuation. This time, the journey was not so spectacular.

On the 18th June, 1940, forty-one children from Northcourt School, which included my brother, my sister and myself, assembled at the Technical Institute, Gravesend. From there we made our way to the nearby Gravesend Central Railway Station, where, our journey to Buckfastleigh in South Devon began. The train took us as far as Newton Abbot. From there we continued by coach to Buckfastleigh.

The small town of Buckfastleigh is situated close to the edge of Dartmoor, and is about ten miles from Newton Abbot. At that time it had a woollen mill, a tannery and several limestone quarries. The lovely River Dart flows nearby and the Dart Valley Railway runs between Buckfastleigh and Totnes.

We were gathered together at the local school, but this time the selection process appeared better organised. People had indicated in advance the sex and number of evacuees they could accommodate.

My sister Betty and I found ourselves in the care of an Irish lady and her family of two daughters and one son. They lived on a council estate on the outskirts of Buckfastleigh. One of the daughters was employed at the local tannery. Because of the limited space in the house, we had to share her bedroom – me sharing a bed with the daughter, and my sister alongside us in a camp bed.

The son of the house kept ferrets, for the purpose of rabbit hunting. This appalled us. We hated the animals, quite apart from the fact that they were rather fierce, and would give one a nasty nip. The lad would take them out of their cages and let them run all over him. We tried not to show fear, but we were absolutely petrified.

For a time, our school was in the basement of a chapel. We had to descend quite a number of stone steps to get to this. The teacher in charge was Mr. Cunningham. He would sit on the edge of a stage at the front of the class, and we would sit at trestle tables. Mr. Cunningham constantly smoked cigarettes from a long cigarette holder, immediately replacing a fresh cigarette each time one had been smoked. He stopped only for his mid-morning cup of Bovril. There was no serious learning, but it was adequate.

A good friend of ours, Gordon, along with three other boys, was billeted with a Major Vickers, a very respected member of the community. He owned a large house in the area, and we would often see him on his horse, with his pack of hounds, gathering for the hunt. It was part of the boys' duties to look after the stables. They lived in part of the servants' quarters, but nevertheless were very happy. It was certainly an insight for the boys into a style of life that had been unfamiliar to them.

Another rather nice large home in the area opened its doors to two other friends. This was owned by a charming lady. She would often allow Betty and I to go to tea with the girls in her lovely house. We spent many happy hours just playing in the spacious grounds of her home.

Doctor Ironside, the local doctor, also took in a little family, two of whom were young twin boys.

My two cousins were accommodated on a farm. They also had their duties on the farm. My brother recalls how, when he used to join them to help during the busy harvesting time, their hard work would be rewarded with frequent welcome drinks of home-made cider. He also recalls how once, quite innocently, he and our two cousins, nearly stopped production at the local woollen mill. They decided to build a dam across a shallow, but swift flowing stream that ran alongside the farm. The three boys had been 'damming' away for some time, when they were approached by an irate gentleman. He asked them to dismantle the dam as they were in danger of 'interfering with the war effort'. They were amazed. What had happened was, they had so skilfully built their dam that they had cut off a vital source of water supply to the mill. The gentleman had re-traced the source from the mill, back along the stream, until he came to the dam. The boys apologised and complied with his demand.

My brother Raymond was billeted with the local butcher, Mr. Hoff, his wife and their son John. It became part of his Saturday job to deliver meat to customers in Buckfastleigh, and the surrounding moorland areas. He would pedal along the road on a trade bicycle with a huge basket, full of meat on the front.

On one of his many trips to the moor to deliver meat, he became aware of a stoat, heading straight for him at a terrific speed. My brother realised that it wasn't going to stop until it had got what it wanted; the meat in his basket. Ray quickly jumped onto the bike, and started to pedal furiously. As he did so, the stoat caught up with him and sank its teeth into the rear tyre of the bicycle. He did not wait to see what would happen next, but just kept pedalling. The stoat eventually let go, but Ray was left with a punctured tyre. The entire incident was a complete revelation to him. He had assumed the only hazards would be from passing vehicles, or from taking a tumble when the heavy amount of meat he carried could cause the cycle to become unstable. It hadn't occurred to him that a small furry animal could home in on the scent of the raw meat; making its soul aim to seek it to eat. From then on, he was always wary when approaching that particular spot.

Another of his escapades again took place on the moor when he was returning after completing his deliveries. As he cycled along, he noticed he had been joined by a pack of Dartmoor ponies. They ran alongside him as he cycled. They looked so tame and inviting. He wondered what it would be like to ride one. He waited until one came abreast of him, then took a flying leap from his cycle onto the unsuspecting pony. The surprised animal shot off, but Ray had anticipated this. He was already clinging very tightly with his arms around the pony's neck. After a while, he realised the animal was not going to stop. He gradually slid his way down the pony's side, still clinging to its neck, and when he saw his chance of a soft landing, he let go. He had achieved what he set out to do without too much upset to the animal, and fortunately, no damage to himself. He picked himself out of the bracken, and feeling very exhilarated, set off back along the road to retrieve his delivery bike.

One of his dislikes, whilst he was staying with the local butcher, was when a truck full of live fowl was delivered. The fowls would have to be slaughtered, and Ray would have to help pluck them to get them ready for sale in the shop. It was so repugnant to him that he became revolted at the thought of eating chicken.

After he had been with the family for some time, it became necessary for him to move, so he went to live with another family where he was quite happy.

During the time that my sister and I were living at our first home in Buckfastleigh, we spent a great deal of our time outdoors, in all weathers. If the weather got too bad, then we would go to the local cinema where it was warm and dry.

As time went by, it became apparent to my mother that we had to move, through information from a visiting neighbour, who had observed our dirty, dishevelled and possibly verminous condition. When she heard this, my mother came to see us and saw that the neighbour was not exaggerating. She took us to the cinema, and whilst we watched the film, she darned the huge holes in our socks. She also replaced missing buttons from our clothes. Her visit resulted in our removal to a local hostel, where we stayed until new accommodation could be found for us. The Evacuee Welfare Lady played a large part in arranging our removal to the hostel, and earned my mother's heartfelt gratitude.

An aunt finally came to our rescue, by offering to look after us until a home could be found for us in Buckfastleigh. She had been evacuated with two children to Regia House, Teignmouth. The entire house was occupied by evacuated families.

My mother managed to make arrangements with another aunt who was serving with the NAAFI at Torquay, to pick us up from Buckfastleigh to accompany us to our new temporary home in Teignmouth.

Regia House was a huge old building, surrounded by a walled garden, and situated very close to the sea. Once inside the front door, we could see a large lounge to our left. This acted as a communal dining-room. To our right there was a long corridor which led to the kitchens. Every family had to do their own cooking. In front of us stretched a very wide staircase. This imposing staircase led to a narrower one. And so it went on, each staircase decreasing in width. Finally, we came to a door at the end of the last passage, which we thought *must* be our room. My aunt opened the door, and to our astonishment, we found ourselves climbing a flight of stairs about two feet wide, which led to three attic rooms. The one my aunt occupied was a long, narrow garret with a very small window. In the corner of the room was a small door, which, if opened, revealed the roof, with many holes where the slates were missing. This garret was to be the bedroom for five of us for a while. It was extremely cold, especially when the snow began to fall. In the past, the attic rooms might have been the servants' quarters.

As one descended from the attic to the ground floor, the rooms got larger. I remember the very sinister thought in my mind created by the sight of the huge, dark polished wooden doors at the entrance to each room. How my spirits lifted each time one opened, and nothing worse than a little family of toddlers came spilling out!

Christmas 1940 coincided with our stay at Regia House. The women got together to give the children a good Christmas. A large tree had been erected in the communal dining room, and a party was arranged. We all contributed to the evening with our own personal party piece.

For a short time, Betty and I attended one of the schools in Teignmouth. We did not like it much. It was strange to us, plus the fact that we had a very long walk to get to it. We invariably lost our way, resulting in our continual unpunctuality. Nobody paid any attention to us and did not even notice if we were there or not.

We did enjoy going down to the beach. A large part of it was cordoned off, but we managed to find a part where the public were allowed to go. We loved to walk around on the wet sand, picking up shells. One day, we collected a whole bag of winkles. We took them back to my aunt and asked her to cook them for us. She had no idea how to cook them, but guessed that just boiling them was all that was needed. They tasted ghastly!

One day, we had a surprise visit from my brother, who was still living in Buckfastleigh. The Evacuee Welfare Lady had brought him to see us. It was her job to keep an eye on all the evacuees, but she always did just that little bit more than what was required of her. She was plump, and motherly, and had as great an affection for us as we had for her. I remember she took my sister to hospital for a check up, after she had suffered a particularly bad bout of tonsilitis. Mrs. Howse made it a really nice day out for her.

During my brother's visit to us at Regia House, we showed him all over the house. Like us, he was not happy being in such close proximity to so many people all under one roof.

Eventually, the time came for our return to Buckfastleigh, and yet another home. I wondered what this one would be like. I was beginning to feel quite befuddled by all the traumatic events which had overtaken my sister and I since we had left Gravesend. Although my aunt had given us a home, we never felt happy living at Regia House. It was not that my aunt hadn't cared for us, she had.

On the day we left Teignmouth, it was pouring with rain. We managed to find Bossell Terrace, a neat row of stone cottages, each with its own unfenced front garden. These were situated behind a large wall with access through a wrought iron gate. Looking soggy, we stood at the door of Number Two, which was to be our new home. A lady opened the door and invited us in, and we were inside a neat, clean little house with a homely atmosphere. She took our coats and cases and introduced herself as Mrs. Coaker. A young lady of about nineteen came into the room. Mrs. Coaker said this was her daughter Joan. We took an instant liking to her. She appeared to be an extremely bright and happy person. Joan told us that her mother was very deaf and we would need to speak up a little. Mrs. Coaker, however, was very adept at lip reading, and we never had difficulty in communicating with her.

After tea, my aunt returned to Teignmouth, and we were left to start another new phase of our lives. Joan showed us the bedroom where we would be sleeping. It contained a double bed, a chest of drawers for our clothes, a few other small items of furniture, and just inside the bedroom door, a very large teddy bear, propped up on a chair. He obviously belonged to Joan, but he was on loan to us throughout our stay.

At day's end, when my sister and I were lying in the double bed, I thought that this place felt right. It was like pouring balm over my troubled mind. Although still a child, I felt these people cared.

We later discovered that a very elderly lady, by the name of Mrs. Haymer, also stayed for long periods of time with Mrs. Coaker and Joan. She told us that she had come from London. She knew what it was like to be an evacuee.

After we had been there a few weeks, a very disturbing episode followed, which I can only think was due to our previous upheavals. Betty and I would retire to bed by candle light quite happily, but for some reason, we would wake up later in sheer terror. We would try to suppress these feelings, but because we could not see one another in the dark, we would get out of bed, hold hands, and just scream until somebody came. It must have been very upsetting for Mrs. Coaker and Joan. The fear we felt was so real. After a while, when we had been re-assured, comforted, and mildly admonished, this very unsettled stage in our lives passed.

We met my brother again and started to make new friends in the immediate vicinity. We now attended the local school. I cannot recall a great deal about it, except that I joined the Scottish country dancing group, which I enjoyed very much.

We spent a lot of time just roaming round the beautiful countryside of South Devon. One day, in the company of my friend and sister, we set out for a walk. We went down through the town, across the Buckfastleigh/Totnes road, and along the banks of the River Dart. We saw before us a very steep, grassy woodland bank. To our utter delight, we could see that it was completely covered in a thick carpet of primroses and violets. I felt I just wanted to wallow in the sight and scent of them. Although we had come from the lovely county of Kent, we had never had such easy access to the beauties of nature. I found myself wishing that my mother could see the glorious sight. I determined I would go back next day to pick some of the flowers to send home to her. I told Mrs. Coaker what we wanted to do. She packed us a picnic basket each, and said the baskets would be useful to put our primroses in. What a lovely afternoon we had. By the time we had finished, our baskets were a mass of tightly packed primroses. We also found some moss which we thought would be good to pack around the flowers when we sent them home. What more contentment can there be than wandering along the celandine strewn banks of the swift-flowing, bubbling River Dart, on a warm sunny afternoon, with the fruits of willing labours packed into a dainty basket? The combined fragrances were heavenly.

Next day, Mrs. Coaker helped us to pack the primroses gently into a box. They were sent to our mother. We later had a letter from her saying how delighted she had been to receive them. For the first time since we had come to Devonshire, we started to attend church regularly. Mrs. Coaker and Joan were Christians, so we were expected to attend church every Sunday. It was the custom in the little town to attend Matins at Holy Trinity, the parish church of Buckfastleigh. Joan would sit in the family pew near the front of the church, with either her friend or her cousin. Although I think Joan would have preferred us to sit near her, where she could keep an eye on us, she very kindly allowed us to sit with our fellow evacuees in the very last pew at the back of the church, which was raised higher than the rest. The fact that each pew had its own little door, was an added attraction to us. I don't think we misbehaved too much, but I know sometimes we would receive a black look from the vicar, the Reverend Millcrease, if we let our minds wander. We tried very hard not to make a noise. With the vicar's sermons, in spite of many tempting diversions, we did try our best to listen to them, as we were all very fond of him.

Just outside the entrance to Holy Trinity church stands a roofed tomb of Richard Cabell. He was thought to be in league with the devil, and to prevent his spirit from haunting the neighbourhood, it was fortified by iron railings. The attraction to us was its unique appearance.

On Sunday afternoons, we attended Sunday School, and on most Sunday evenings, we would attend Evensong at another church in the town. Here, for some unknown reason, we would all sit at the front of the church. It was a smaller, more modern church, and the same vicar administered to both churches. My brother was a choir boy, and whilst we were living in Buckfastleigh, he was confirmed into the Church of England. The Choirmaster and Organist was Mr. Penny, and sometimes he could be heard during the service calling to a tired or forgetful choir boy, to pump more wind into the slowing organ!

One rather sorrowful event at the church on the hill, was the funeral of one of our fellow evacuees. His name was Sydney Parker, aged about ten, who unfortunately died after having pneumonia. His small coffin was borne from the church to the graveside by his friends from the school, one of whom was my brother. It took us a long time to get over this tragedy.

If it was a nice sunny day, we would climb the hill to the church to visit the little boy's grave, then perhaps descend over one hundred stone steps behind the churchyard down to Buckfast Abbey.

Buckfast Abbey was, and still is, a most beautiful building. Built and still run by monks of the Benedictine Order it was started in 1907 and completed in 1938. The local limestone from which it is built appears to glow brightly in the sunshine. The stained glass windows were made by the monks.

When we first visited the abbey, as young children, we were fascinated by the little piscina just inside the main door. We were told that it contained holy water. People of the Catholic faith, before entering the body of the abbey, anointed themselves from it with the sign of the cross. As we were of the Church of England faith, this was not our custom, but we decided as we were in a Catholic building, out of respect, we should do the same.

The monks always found time for us, and would answer our many and varied questions, despite the fact that they were constantly busy working around the grounds. An example of their hospitality and kindness was shown to my brother whenever he had to deliver meat to them. They would insist that he sat at their table to eat a bowl of hot soup and bread, before continuing with his deliveries. He looked forward to his visits there. As well as working in the grounds, the monks had a small shop attached to the abbey where they sold honey, produced from their own beehives. Over the years, they have become renowned world wide for their Buckfast Tonic Wine and their expertise in stained glass, pottery and carvings.

Whenever my mother and father came to see us, we loved to take them to Buckfast Abbey. I have since been back several times, and it is still the same beautiful place.

One of the regular weekly events we looked forward to was receiving our pocket money from our mother. We had to buy National Savings stamps with half of it, but the rest we were allowed to spend as the fancy took us. Sweets were purchased from the little shop in town which was owned by a pleasant elderly lady.

Opposite the sweet shop was a drapery shop. My sister and I would stand gazing into the window at the display; pretty ribbons, cottons, silks, thimbles, brooches, and handkerchiefs. One day, whilst window gazing, I spotted a pale blue brush and comb set in a blue 'leather' case. I thought this was beautiful, and longed to be able to buy it for my mother. I was afraid that it would be far too expensive. However, I plucked up courage to go inside to ask the price. My fears were confirmed. I was just about to leave the shop when the assistant, seeing my disappointment, called me back. She said if I promised to call in and pay her something each week until it was paid for, she would keep it for me. I welcomed my arranged visit each week as it gave me chances to explore this 'Aladdin's Cave'. When I had completed the payments I felt so proud of my purchase – quite the most expensive thing I had ever bought. As anticipated, my mother liked it very much, and kept it for many years.

Another place we liked to visit was a nearby farm where we used to buy cream by the jug full. This was kept in a large, stone out-house building, very primitive and bare, but also very clean. Inside the building were several large stone slabs, about table height, and on these stood large shallow bowls full of milk. Each bowl was at a different stage in the creaming process. Taking our jug, a lady would go to one of the large bowls with a huge ladle, drain off the excess milk, and then pour the ladle full of rich cream into it. It was always very cool in this building, and a delightful place to be, especially on a hot day. Never since have I tasted cream quite like it.

After my father's return from Dunkirk, he was stationed at Lechlade in Gloucestershire. For a while my mother joined him there. Sometimes he was able to pay us a quick visit. Whenever he and my mother came, they tried to make their visit as interesting as possible. If the weather was good, we would go walking on the moors which edged Buckfastleigh. Mrs. Coaker would pack us a picnic, and include some of her home-made elderberry or elderflower wine. It was delicious. We would ramble for hours through the heather and bracken. If we were lucky, we would find a suitable brook to paddle in, before sitting down to enjoy our picnic.

On another visit, my father hired a car with a driver from a garage in Buckfastleigh, so that we could travel a little further afield. We felt very grand having our very own 'chauffeur'. First, we went to see various places on Dartmoor. He pointed out Dartmoor Prison, which we thought looked a very grey and lonely place. At Postbridge we saw the old clapper bridge. This was a primitive, ancient bridge of stone slabs, each about two feet wide – just wide enough for a man or a horse to cross. My brother got so excited about this place that he fell into the river. But it was shallow. He was soon fished out, dried off, and our journey continued. Nothing was going to stop us that day! We went next to Kingsteignton, to visit the parents of one of my father's army colleagues. During the war, people were grateful to receive first hand news of their loved ones. They were a charming couple and made us all feel welcome. After staying for a time, we went on to Torquay to visit Kent's Caverns. I had no idea what to expect here and felt a little apprehensive when I realised we had to go deep below ground. However, as we descended, we saw a magnificent group of prehistoric caves of stalactites and stalagmites. These were lit from behind to show off their beauty. It was very cold and unreal. I imagined it must be like walking on another planet. When we returned to the surface, my father asked a passer-by to take a photograph of our family.

Going back to Buckfastleigh, we mulled over the events of the day. We laughed about Ray's ducking in the River Dart at Postbridge; recalled the happy hours we had spent in Kingsteignton with the parents of my father's colleague, and marvelled at the wonderful places we had seen during the day. We had had a perfect day.

We re-lived this day over and over again in our memories. Before much more time had elapsed, we learnt that my father was to be posted to India. We were shattered at the prospect, but my mother must have felt devastated.

My mother and father talked over the family situation, and decided that it would be best if we returned to Gravesend. By April 1942, arrangements were made for my uncle to come to Buckfastleigh to escort the three of us home. We said our goodbyes to Joan and Mrs. Coaker. Although I know my uncle would have fully passed on my mother's thanks, I only hope we were thoughtful enough to adequately thank the Coakers for giving us a home, and for sharing so much of their lives with us.

Epilogue

During the course of the years that followed, I made several visits to Norfolk and Devonshire. I had the pleasure of seeing the Smiths and the Coakers again.

My mother's thoughts were never expressed to me until many years after the war. She told me that after seeing us off from Gravesend on the morning of September 3rd, 1939, she returned home. She entered the house, where only a few hours earlier there had been three chattering children, all demanding her immediate attention. Now, there was only the dog – Topsy – to greet her. She tried to come to terms with the situation. She wondered if her decision to let us go had been wise.

She allowed herself a brief moment to weep the tears she had for so long withheld. As if to comfort her, the dog tried to lick the tears from her cheeks. When she received the official card telling her where we were, she felt happier. She wrote to us every week and sent us pocket money and replacement clothes when necessary. She also came to see us as often as possible.

When we returned home in 1942, she had to learn to cope with three (almost) teenage children, but that created no problem. We were soon back to being a family again. Our joy of returning home was marred by the fact that our father was posted to India. He stayed for the next three years. My brother and I continued our education at a senior school and my sister returned to the junior school. We each joined a youth organisation, the Girl Guides, the Brownies, the Boy Scouts. We coped extremely well with the remainder of the bombing raids; the V1s (Doodlebugs) and the V2 rockets.

When my father returned to this country in 1945 and was demobbed from the Army, for a while we felt strange. We were even shy, at having a man around the house. I recall my father saying he had not realised that my brother and I had grown into young adults whilst he had been away. His memories of us had been as young children. My mother had performed the role of mother and father extremely well. She had been responsible for all decision making and discipline. I know she was very happy when my father was once again able to share that responsibility with her.

These are my personal sentiments regarding the virtues, or otherwise, of evacuation. I have been asked, so many times, if I would have agreed to a child of mine taking part in the evacuation. I have reservations.

If one was lucky enough to be accommodated in an agreeable environment with an understanding and sympathetic family, then the degree of stress on a child's mind was minimal. But in the absence of the 'agreeable' factors, the stress could be extremely great. I was nine years old at the time of the evacuation. A child at that time was very innocent, compared to today's nine year olds. I picked up snippets of conversation, either from the media or an individual, regarding the ruthless deeds of our 'enemy'. I knew my mother was still living in the place that had been considered unsafe for us. As a result, I imagined all sorts of terrible things were happening to her. Had I not been evacuated, then I would have had the ordeal of coping with the air raids. But, because we would have been together, I know my anxiety would have been lessened. This fact was confirmed for me when we finally returned home to spend the second half of the war years in Gravesend.

Having said this, the Irish family aside, my thanks are owed to the good people of Norfolk and Devon. They provided the 'agreeable' factors for me. I survived, along with many others, and today, am none the worse for the ordeal. My brother, my sister and myself have our mixed bag of some sad, but mostly happy memories. Given a choice, I probably would not have gone. But at nine years old, I was incapable of making a rational decision. Our parents took that decision for us. In their view, it was the one best for us. They were not alone in making that decision. They wanted us to have a future. Had we stayed, we might not have had one.

Christine Gardener now lives in Deal near Dover in Kent. She is married with a grown up family and works on a voluntary basis in a charity shop for the Children's Society.

41

B.

DEFENCE REGULATIONS

To _____
(Name)

Occupier of _____
(Address)

_____

    In pursuance of the Defence Regulations, I hereby require you to provide, in the above mentioned premises, accommodation for the following persons :—

_____

_____

_____

_____

_____

_____

ADULTS _____   CHILDREN UNDER 14 _____

      Signed _____
                                       Billeting Officer.

Date of Billeting _____

Instructions to Occupiers

    You are required to provide, until further notice, in the premises described above accommodation, consisting of shelter and reasonable access to water supply and sanitary conveniences, for the persons hereby assigned to those premises. *Should you fail to carry out this requirement you will commit an offence.*

    You cannot charge any person so assigned for the accommodation which you are required to provide, but you will receive payment in respect thereof at the rate of

                                                                      *

_____

per week, being 5/- per week in respect of each adult and 3/- per week in respect of each child under 14. Payment will be made weekly, in advance, at the

_____ †Post Office on presentation of this form, commencing on the date of billeting.

    You are not required by law to provide facilities for cooking, but it is hoped that you will do so.

    If you have good cause to do so, you may apply to the Billeting Officer to relieve you of the above requirement to provide accommodation.

*Total amount payable to be written in words by the Billeting Officer.
†To be filled in by the Occupier (payee).

The first defence regulations made it clear that accommodation for evacuees should consist of shelter and reasonable access to water and sanitary conveniences. The provider was paid the princely sum of 5/- per adult and 3/- per child per week.

DEFENCE REGULATIONS

To ....

     (Name)

Occupier of ....

     (Address)

....

    In pursuance of the Defence Regulations, I hereby require you to provide, in the above-mentioned premises, board and lodging for the following person :

Signed..

                          Billeting Officer.

Date of Billeting...

INSTRUCTIONS TO OCCUPIERS.

    You are required to provide, until further notice, in the premises described above, board and lodging for the person hereby assigned to those premises. *Should you fail to carry out this requirement you will commit an offence.*

    You cannot charge any person so assigned for the accommodation which you are required to provide, but you will receive payment in respect thereof at the rate of twenty-one shillings per week in respect of this person.

    Payment will be made weekly, in advance, at the .... *
Post Office on presentation of this form, commencing on the date of billeting.

    A tribunal has been constituted to deal with complaints against billeting notices. If you feel aggrieved by the service upon you of this notice, you may lodge a complaint, which should be addressed to the offices of the Local Authority.

    THIS FORM MUST BE SURRENDERED TO THE BILLETING OFFICER IMMEDIATELY THE ABOVE-MENTIONED PERSON CEASES TO BE BILLETED ON YOU.

       * To be filled in by the Occupier (Payee).

The second set of regulations gave the provider of accommodation somewhat more money (21/- per week per person) but the requirements were now for board and lodgings.

The Mayor and Mayoress of Gravesend sent Christmas greetings to evacuees in Norfolk.

44

The Eatwell family, during the war. Pat the youngest of four children is fourth from the left.

Garth, the house at Binfield to which Pat Eatwell was evacuated, pictured in 1981. The copper beech (foreground) was still there.

"Garth"
by
PAT EATWELL

I WAS born in Croydon, the youngest of four children. Our family life was probably typical of many there, happy, carefree to a degree and sometimes noisy. I was 11 when this life-style was to change completely after that one short sentence, heard over the radio, announced that we were at war with Germany.

Miss Collinson was someone I had only seen once or twice. It was she who sent me a gift each birthday, and to whom I wrote

a 'thank you' letter the next day. She had been one of the volunteer nurses abroad in the First World War. When my Dad was injured, she had taken him, along with other soldiers, to her father's estate in Wales to convalesce. They had kept in touch throughout the years, and she had asked to be my godmother when I was born. This lady had now written and offered to have me to live with her at Binfield, should war come.

My first feeling, on being told of my evacuation, I suppose, was excitement at the prospect of living in the country. I don't think my thoughts went any further than that, but I have to say that the short while I spent with her certainly made an impression on me, and was a time I will remember all my life.

As we drove through the countryside, I was immediately struck by the little lanes where the trees, heavy with leaves, formed arches above us. I remember thinking it was like fairyland. We arrived at the house, which was called "Garth". I just couldn't believe my eyes. At home we had a small house directly onto the road, and here was a beautiful creeper covered house (2 cottages converted) with a drive, lots of flowers and trees. One of the trees I fell in love with immediately, learning later that it was a copper beech. This was to be my home?

A maid opened the door and I met Miss Collinson. I was then introduced to her housekeeper, Miss Huggins, and we were shown over the house. The rooms, even to my young eyes, were lovely.

It appeared there was a different room for each use, not just a living room where the whole family did everything together, but a drawing room, a dining-room, a study with lots of books and a big rambling kitchen. My bedroom was at the top of the stairs, with my own little bed (at home I shared a big bed with my two sisters). There was also my own dressing table, wardrobe, washstand with a big jug and basin, matching soapdish and toothbrush holder, and joy of joys, a carpeted floor.

Before Mum and Dad left I was told the house rules. I would be woken at 7.30am with hot water to wash in (this would make a change from running on cold lino down to the scullery), and I was to be downstairs at 8 am prompt on school days with everything I needed for school as I was not to go running up and down stairs wearing out the carpet. Twice a day would be allowed, and during the day I would use the outside lavatory. I would have all my meals in the kitchen with Miss Huggins and Emily, except on Sundays when I would take lunch and an early dinner in the dining room with Miss Collinson.

That first evening my little bedroom wasn't such a joy after all. I was alone for the first time in my life, and everywhere was so quiet. No sounds of radio or people talking, no traffic. I felt very scared at the thought of living there, added to which big blackout curtains were drawn against the window, and I kept thinking I had gone blind. I was lonely and unhappy and cried myself to sleep.

The next afternoon Miss Collinson took me to the local school where the headmaster bowed to her. This puzzled me. He assured her I would be well looked after and suggested the names of some children suitable to be my friends. She apparently agreed these, and we were taken to meet my class. I remember feeling silly when he told them that they had a special girl starting school tomorrow. He made them all stand up and say "Good afternoon Pat".

The next day when I started school, Emily walked me there. The headmaster met us at the gate and took me in. I was introduced to my 'friends' – no more rough and tumble in the playground for me, they seemed too ladylike. But one of those girls, Bridget, did become my best friend. It was with her that I walked to and from school, sometimes stopping at The Lodge where she lived to play for a while. Then I would tidy myself up, comb my hair and walk the last yards home very demurely. One day at school a girl asked if I was gentry because her Dad had said I was. As I'd never heard the word I said I didn't know. I didn't like the sound of it though and asked when I arrived home. Miss Huggins told me "No, you most certainly are not, but make sure you behave as if you were". I was then no wiser.

My days became a pattern which was rigidly adhered to. Each school morning, before leaving, I would go up to Miss Collinson's room where she would be having her breakfast on a tray. She would tell me to fetch the biscuit caddy from the corner table, take out two biscuits which she gave to me for my school lunch. I don't know why, but I always had the feeling I should act surprised, and so I did – every day!

Every evening, at 5.30 exactly, I would be called into the drawing room where Miss Collinson was to teach me to play the piano. I had to do one hour's practice at this time each day. Then at 6.30 we would sit opposite each other and knit khaki socks or balaclava helmets for the soldiers. During this time, Miss Collinson would ask me about school that day, and correct my speech and accent. Sometimes there would be a basket of washed bandages delivered which we would sort and rewind. At 7.30 I would be sent back to the kitchen for milk and a piece of cake, and 8.15 to bed.

On my way to bed, I had to go into the dining room to say goodnight. Miss Collinson always wore a long dress for dinner, even though alone, and had on earrings and a necklace. I always thought she looked so elegant sitting at the beautifully laid table, always with fresh flowers.

49

Each Saturday morning I was allowed to sit at the big, bureau in the study to write a letter home, I was allowed to use a big black metal stamp which indented the address onto the first page. I felt so important. I was also able to enjoy the garden at weekends. At home, we had only a small back yard to play in. Here there were two big lawns, one set out for croquet, and one surrounded by bushes and trees with the kitchen garden beyond. It was here that I first smelled new mown grass. Another first was to sit and read with just the rustle of trees and birds singing. Even now, these things always take me back to "Garth".

I enjoyed Sunday afternoons when we would play croquet, if fine, or ludo in the drawing room in front of the fire if it was cold. Sunday dinner, however, was my worst time. At home I had never thought about the origin of the meat on my plate – I hadn't seen animals in the fields, or chickens. I can still remember the sick feeling I had when the gardener brought a still warm chicken into the kitchen and told me this was to be my dinner the next day. We also had rabbit, pigeon, pheasant and grouse, all of which I hated. As I had to clear my plate, I became very adept at swallowing the meat whole and making a big thing of chewing the vegetables. It was alright during the week, because although Miss Huggins would tut if I didn't like the meat, she would take it off my plate and divide it between herself and Emily. I have never eaten poultry or game since.

At Christmas, the school was putting on the play "Sleeping Beauty", and I was to be the princess (not for any artistic prowess) but because Mum and Dad had been invited as special guests. As it was to be in the evening, Miss Collinson suggested that Mum should stay in the guest room, but not my Dad, even though it was a double room. I can still hear her saying, "You will appreciate I'm sure Perry (our surname) that I have never had a man stay in my house, and I have only one bathroom". He put up at the local inn down the road, but I felt so sorry for my Mum, because I know she really felt out of place. Such was my godmother's logic. I can understand her view now but at the time it didn't make sense to me at all.

I went home for Easter as the dreaded air raids hadn't materialised, and on the day before I was due back, came out in a lovely rash of measles. By the time I had recovered, my parents had decided to keep me with them at home. I never went back to Binfield. Apparently the first words I said on being told this decision was "Good, now I won't have to eat 'peasant' ever again".

Now having had a family of my own, I feel very sad that at the time, I never gave enough thought to all the people involved. My parents for letting me go, but also for Miss Collinson who, bless her heart, up until then had been a happy spinster; living her quiet uncomplicated life. Yet she had volunteered to take the responsibility for a little urchin – I know I was no angel. I thought my life had turned upside down on the day I was evacuated, but I dread to think what the upheaval must have done to hers. I shall always be grateful to her, she helped me to grow up. I will always remember "Garth", with its beautiful gardens, with utmost love and affection.

Pat Eatwell's family left Croydon and moved to Borstal near Rochester in Kent when she was 15 years old. She has lived there ever since. Pat is now a widow with three children. She retired in 1987 after a career with IPC magazines.

Fifty Years On
by
NORA FRY

IT IS amazing to recall that the evacuation of children took place 51 years ago. It is an event which I can remember quite clearly. Actually, the arrangements began in 1938. I was at Rochester Grammar School, then 13, and my sister Eileen was 8. Our parents decided then that we should stay together and arrangements were made. The grammar school would include younger brothers and sisters in their evacuation plans. Then we had

the famous "Peace in our time" statement, but my father never believed it. As a keen follower of current events, he thought war was inevitable.

For the first time in years we were to go on holiday. This was in August 1939, and we went to Hythe. My father vowed he would not buy a paper or listen to the radio that week! Wednesday was my 14th birthday and we all went to see the Hythe Grand Venetian Fete, a wonderful spectacle of decorated and illuminated boats on the Royal Military Canal. It was our last happy day as a family for some years as it turned out. By Thursday it wasn't possible to ignore the news any longer. A telephone call home made it clear that if Eileen and I were to join the grammar school party we would have to go home the next day, and join a tail-enders party on Saturday. Back through Kent on the double decker bus we went through villages where the London children were already arriving by the coach load. Sad little groups clutching carrier bags, and looking bewildered as harrassed adults tried to sort them out. We knew this was how we would be the next day!

So it was as we went to Rochester station, and joined the late party. There were mainly expectant mums and a few stragglers like us. Going on the train was exciting, not something we did very often. I'm not sure at that point we even knew where we were going. I know I regarded it as quite an adventure as we waved goodbye – only many years later, after my mother had died, did I find her diary with the entry that day, "This is the worst day of my life". At 14, I thought it exciting!

We ended up in Canterbury. At the station we were given a tin of corned beef, a tin of condensed milk and some biscuits, to help out our hostess. Next we were marched off to the Simon Langton School which was then in the middle of the High Street. It was a long wait, as the expectant mums were dealt with first. All the excitement was replaced with uncertainty. At last it was our turn. An elderly lady came over, and told us briskly to collect our bags and follow her. We got into a car – that was unusual too – and drove off to her house.

I'm not sure at what point I made the discovery that she was the headmistress of the Simon Langton Grammar School for Girls, Miss Campling. She lived in quite a palatial house – by my standards – in St. Augustines Road. Furthermore she had a maid, Lilian. The whole set-up was suddenly frightening! Headmistresses were held in a good deal of awe then and it was like being in school 24 hours a day, always on your best behaviour.

The next day was Sunday and we joined our school party outside Canterbury Cathedral for the morning service. The big west doors were open, horses drawing carts piled high with earth were going in and dumping the earth across the main nave, and the precious stained glass windows were being carefully removed. We went down into the crypt which was crowded. I think the sermon was given by Dr. Hewlett

Johnson, famously known as the "Red Dean". I am uncertain about this, but I believe at 11 there was a radio so we could hear the Prime Minister's statement. The words he used were something like this, "I have to tell you that no such assurance has been given and that therefore we are at war with Germany". There was complete silence for a few minutes. Before anyone could say any thing more the alert sounded!

We had heard this before, in practice, but this time we thought it was for real! I clasped my sister's hand, everyone stayed calm, and I suppose we were in a pretty good place, sheltered from anything bar a direct hit. I don't think it lasted long before the "All Clear" sounded and we came out into the sunshine of the Precincts. Nothing had changed! I remember feeling quite astounded, war had been declared, the alert had gone, and people stood around talking just like we always did after morning service.

We were in Canterbury, what was going to happen to us next? I don't think that had been very well thought out, because we were sent to work in the hop fields! No schooling had been organised for us, so while this was being sorted out, off we all went everyday to work with the hoppers – who were not best pleased! After all, none of us had done this before, so we weren't very quick and we were given to the regular London hoppers who had done it all their lives and were quick at stripping the bines. They earned money doing it – we of course did not! We must have spent 5-6 hours a day in the fields, my lasting impression was how stained and green my fingers got, I never seemed able to get it off at the end of the day, and the smell was quite strong too, something our hostess didn't like!

This went on for several weeks, until my sister along with several others attached to the school were put into an infants school, and so were we! An infants school at the end of Broad Street. Imagine us getting our 14-15 year old bottoms in those dinky little baby chairs, the ones with rounded seats and arms! We didn't fit very well, and although it gave us a lot of laughs getting stuck, I think we must have been fairly unruly! At last we were accommodated in the "Old Hospital", recently vacated. Gradually desks came, staff appeared, and lessons began to get some degree of normality. We shared this with the Maths School, Rochester and a London Boys school. Hours were very erratic.

Meanwhile, back at the billet life was tricky. Really we were happier in the kitchen with Lilian the maid, but we had to dine, while Lilian served us. One of our big treats at home was eating in a Lyons Corner House, but nothing had prepared us for this. At home, our father always took tea time as an opportunity to explain to us current affairs to help with homework. Here we weren't allowed to talk at all, and not allowed to have an opinion about anything. We certainly weren't allowed to be homesick, why should we be? Miss Campling told our mother it was not necessary to come and see us, once she knew we were alright. It is no wonder that Eileen and I cried ourselves to sleep most nights!

A number of children went home very soon, but father was made of sterner stuff. He was sure the blow would fall eventually, and we must be safe. Before Christmas came we were moved into a temporary billet, while a more home-like place was found for us. Of course, we weren't to be separated so finding someone who would take two children wasn't so easy. After a few weeks we moved again, this time to a family with two girls. Although they were a bit older than Eileen and I, it had a very different atmosphere to the grand house we had been in. Miss Campling had enormous experience with girls 'en masse', but with two homesick youngsters, who needed re-assurance and a bit of mothering, this was really beyond her.

Despite all the difficulties, we had a very good Christmas – all provided at the school. We had an excellent Christmas dinner, so we ate Mum's Christmas pudding the next day. People invited us out to tea, and a grand meal was given to us all at the Baptist Chapel. At the weekend, our parents came for the day. As I recorded in my diary, the end of the year finished up very well!

Looking at this diary, I regret to say I really didn't record anything about the reason we were in Canterbury. We went to school, many of the grammar school staff were with us, only a few stayed behind in Rochester to give schooling to those still there. I did record I had a boyfriend, well, at 14 that was vital wasn't it! The big event at the end of February was that Eileen and I were allowed to go home for a week. My mother came to fetch us. Soon we were back with all our family – it was marvellous. All our aunts and uncles appeared and our cousins, and best of all our grandma. She was a lively, story-telling 70 year old, whose tales of the 1914 war seemed much more interesting than the one that was going on now! All too soon our week was up, and we were back in Canterbury, with the promise that we could go home at Easter, which we did.

We had begun to think this was all that was going to happen to us and the war would soon be over. In any event we were to go home again for Whitsun. And then everything changed. On May 9th, the Germans began their advance. On the 10th, Belgium and Holland were invaded. During the next week, the epic evacuation of Dunkirk took place. We were not able to go home, and I remember it as a time of great confusion. I had two uncles, one in the RAF and one in the Guards. We had no idea what had happened to them, although thankfully, they did both get away. As the Germans raced towards the Channel ports, Canterbury was a good deal less safe. On the 17th of May we were told we were going to South Wales. I suppose our parents were informed, for the next day mine came down and my mother was asked if she would like to join the school party, as a 'helper'. She must have felt very torn, as the war had now started in earnest, and I think it must have been Daddy who made the choice for her. He had to stay at home, partly for his job, and because he was a Sergeant in the Home Guard. They might have a vital role to play. So, after frantically packing all our possessions we were marched up to Canterbury station on Sunday May 19th, and headed for Pontypridd, in South Wales. This was the longest journey we had ever undertaken and it would have been quite frightening if our mother had not been with us.

It was a bright and sunny day, but our train was frequently stopped as troop trains had a greater priority than ours. As the troops came back from Dunkirk, all the units were scattered and had to be re-assembled. We waved to everyone that passed us. We left Canterbury at about 8 and didn't get to Pontypridd until about 5. We were grateful for the sandwiches we had packed.

When we arrived what a welcome we got! On the platform was the town band, a choir, and the Mayor. They really were delighted to see us. We got biscuits, chocolate, tinned meat, tea, all given by the townspeople, many of whom were waiting outside to wave and cheer us. We were taken to local junior schools, and gradually found billets. Our was with Mrs Davies, who made a great fuss of us. Despite the fact that we must have arrived at very short notice, and they were expecting under 11's, the next day arrangements had been made for us to share the local girls' grammar school. I had been introduced to the girl who would take me there – Betty Jones – and we became firm friends. Now 50 years on, we still are!

Pontypridd lies in the Taff valley, among the mountains of South Wales. I thought it was beautiful even though it was a mining town. But it had attractive public gardens and tennis courts. The school was on the outskirts of the town and meant a walk over the mountains. It too had spacious grounds and a well-designed building.

In common with the rest of South Wales, this area was only just recovering from the depression following the miner's strike of 1924, and the closure of many pits. I was told later that the money that the evacuees brought into the town – in the form of lodging allowances and personal spending money – gave a boost to the economy, which had been sadly lacking for many years. We shared the school, and then used church halls for the rest of the day. We were able to go swimming, and to play tennis.

I wrote to my father and begged for a tennis racquet, as my 15th birthday was coming up. To my delight he sent me the money and I bought a Dunlop and a frame for 18/- (90p). But it really was quite a lot of money then. I don't know if it improved my game, but it certainly encouraged me to play a lot! By this time we really felt at home. We were having to work quite hard, as we only had a year before we were to sit the London University School Certificate exams, much like the GCSE is now. Then we heard that the other half of the school left in Rochester had been sent to Porthcawl, a town on the coast about 30 miles away. We had frequent air raid alerts, mainly as the German planes flew over to bomb the Midlands and spent quite a lot of time sitting in the corridors at school, or out of bed downstairs. In Kent we had had air raid shelters, but I suppose nobody thought they were necessary here. Although bombs were dropped, they were usually jettisoned ones, as aircraft flew home after their mission.

My memories of Pontypridd are all happy ones. First of all, mother was with us, we had a comfortable billet, and I had made friends with several local girls who all went to the grammar school that we shared. My sister went to the school just across the road and we were welcome everywhere. Then a blow fell. On the 10th July, we were told we were all being sent to Porthcawl, where the rest of the school were billeted.

This was really very sad, just as we had thought we were settled, to have to move again. It did prove to be very unsettling, and I never felt as happy there as I had in Pontypridd. I don't think any of us did, we always seemed to be changing billets, school hours, church halls, and we still had our exams to take. In fact, we were in the middle of doing some when on Sunday July 14th we left for Porthcawl.

It all started badly. I suppose there were over 100 girls, plus luggage. We arrived at the school at 10, and the coaches were late. When we reached our billet it was after 4, we had had no lunch and none was ready for us – and of course we were starving! We had been put into a large boarding house, about 10 of us, including Mummy and we were packed in. I can only suppose the owner wanted to make up for her lost summer customers. We got very little to eat and of course we all hated it. Luckily, with Mummy there, getting everyone moved out proved not too difficult.

The next week she found rooms for us. We had two rooms, which meant we had to sleep in one of them and a sitting room which we more or less had to ourselves. Mummy did most of the cooking. She spent most of her day at school, doing clerical work, checking girls not at school, taking others to the dentist or the doctor. She was paid for this, so I suppose this was how we managed to pay for the rooms. This time our school was in a very nice secondary modern school, shared, and the rest of the time in an assortment of church halls. We were still doing the inevitable exams. However we managed must remain a mystery!

Sirens sounded quite frequently, so afternoons were spent seated in the corridors, interrupting what schooling we were getting, and nights downstairs, on the floor. Several things were memorable. The Pavilion at Porthcawl provided a lot of entertainment for us. We were allowed to go and see productions like the Welsh Male Voice choirs, and some plays. The highlight was when Dame Sybil Thorndyke and Sir Lewis Casson visited us. Dame Sybil was an old girl of our school, her father having been a Canon at Rochester Cathedral. The first time they performed Shaw's Candida and Macbeth, and on their return, Major Barbara. When the performance was over, we gave her a big bouquet of flowers in the school colours, and went backstage to meet her. Great excitement!

On Saturdays we were allowed to go to the Pavilion so long as Mummy was with us. We could sit in the balcony, while everyone else danced down below. We got to recognise many of the regulars, and the local girls who had new boyfriends each week. One of the boys from the Maths school was allowed in the interval to play the drums. We applauded wildly. His name was Ronnie Verral, and eventually he became the drummer in the Ted Heath Band. He was named Drummer of the Year many times and still plays. I've seen him often in the background on T.V.

At last, at Christmas, my father was able to come and see us. We were so glad to see him because during all this time the Battle of Britain had been fought over Kent, and the threat of invasion was still there. Like all men over military age, he had to carry on with his job, train, and do night duties with the Home Guard. Of course he wrote to us often, but was always very careful about what he said. News bulletins only told us so much, imagination supplied the rest! I think the few days he was able to spend with us must have been a very welcome break for him.

Some of the girls were beginning to drift back home, but most of the staff were still in Porthcawl, and the London University School Certificate exams were beginning to get even closer. In May, 1941 we moved again, this time we had two rooms, and the sitting room was ours alone. I don't think we left our other digs with any bad feelings, but we had been there nearly a year, and our landlady just wanted the house to herself again. It was never foreseen that we would be away so long, and I think all of us had several moves, probably all for the same reason.

Looking back, I think much credit must go to our school staff. We did not have much of the equipment we would have had at our own grammar school, our days were always fragmented, with air raid sirens, being moved in the school, then in church halls. Nevertheless, our Historical Society still ran, and I became the secretary. I am not sure what I did, but I know I was thrilled to be doing it! We put on several plays, "1066 and all that" and some one act plays. We were able to play hockey in the winter and tennis in the summer. A swim on the hot days, on the beaches at Porthcawl was lovely.

At the beginning of July we took our exams, and I have often wondered what allowances were made for us. Not much in the science exam it seems as, without any equipment, we all failed! My father came down in August, and it was decided that Mummy and Eileen would go back with him, I was to remain, and go into the 6th form, there wasn't one at Rochester. My mother found a billet for me, and at first all seemed well, but in fact it turned out to be the worst one I ever had.

My landlady was quite young, with a rather elderly husband and a small daughter aged about 5. She was lazy. I did the washing, cooking and cleaning either before I went to school, or when I came home. Another girl came to join me, so at least we did it together! If we didn't do the housework we lived in a tip, and if we didn't do the cooking we had nothing to eat. We hated to complain, but matters came to a head when I fainted at school. It all had to be revealed – we were both starving! There was a big row, and we were hastily removed!

By this time, I knew I had passed most of my exams, and decision time about what I was to do was drawing near. In the meantime, more staff were going back to Rochester, as that was now the biggest part of the school. I can remember taking the young ones for reading lessons, and quite often supervising their work. My new billet was much nicer, an elderly couple who made quite a fuss of me. When I went home for Christmas, they gave me all sorts of goodies which they had hoarded, since 1939, to give us a good time. I had decided I would like to be a librarian, and tried hard while I was home to find a vacancy. There weren't any, and I finished up going into the Civil Service.

So in January 1942 I went back to Porthcawl, packed my bags, said goodbye to my hostess, and my school friends and after 2½ years, went back home. Was it all worth it? It is hard to say. The war did not start as everyone had expected, on day one with air raids. Neither did it finish as was also expected, before Christmas. In retrospect Canterbury did seem an odd choice to evacuate us to. It was a lot nearer to the continent than Rochester, and in the end, had some very severe air raids which destroyed its city centre. Few arrangements had been made when we arrived; hop picking was thrown in just to keep us occupied! The hurried dash to Pontypridd was as the Germans invaded Holland, and it was suddenly realised that Canterbury was no longer safe.

The shift to Porthcawl was also an improvisation when it was seen that more than half the school had gone there. The school was now in three sections – which must have been quite unworkable.

I am sure that no one had foreseen that the war would last as long as it did or that it was impossible to keep children away without them becoming very homesick. The hostesses would get fed up with having them – not because they were unfeeling or the children naughty – but really because it became clear it was all going to last a very long time.

After I came home, it was not too long that all the school came back to Rochester. My sister, who went to the grammar school in 1943, had a full complement of staff there.

The evacuation disrupted our young lives, but then war disrupted everyone's lives. Being young, we probably adapted much quicker. Eventually all the children drifted back.

It seems odd to remember that when the heavy air raids began over Kent, and we spent night after night in the Anderson shelters, I don't recall any suggestion that the children should be evacuated again – they just took their chance with everyone else!

Norah Fry *still lives in Rochester, Kent and is married to a former Olympic athlete. (Her husband carried the torch in the 1948 Olympics in London and is now a Rochester on Medway Borough Councillor). Mrs Fry is a former civil servant and has a grown up family.*

Norah and her friend Muriel (right).

Form Va Rochester Grammar School July 31st, 1940 at Rest Bay Porthcawl after swimming during the holidays.

Memories of Porthcawl.

Nora Fry wrote: "Hunting for old photos, I found this verse that Eileen, Mummy and I had written while sitting up in the balcony at the Pavilion, Eileen and I still know it off by heart and still have a giggle over it!

> We go to the Pavilion on Saturday nights
> To sit and gaze at Porthcawl's awful sights,
> There's Bonnie Prince Charlie and young Mrs Jones,
> And a long lanky chap who is minus his bones.
> There's a terrible band that is all out of tune,
> And a fat ginger crooner who's lost all his croon,
> His rendering of 'Playmates' is really a scream,
> It's either a nightmare or else a bad dream.
> With pardon-me-foxtrots and waltzes galore
> They hop skip and shuffle all over the floor.
> But it keeps us all merry and makes us feel bright
> To go to the Pavilion on Saturday nights!

Poets we were not but we always had a good time there."

Mrs. Smith and her brother George gave a home to Christine Gardener and her friend Masie. They are pictured here with Christine's father (in uniform), her sister Betty (front) and her brother Raymond.

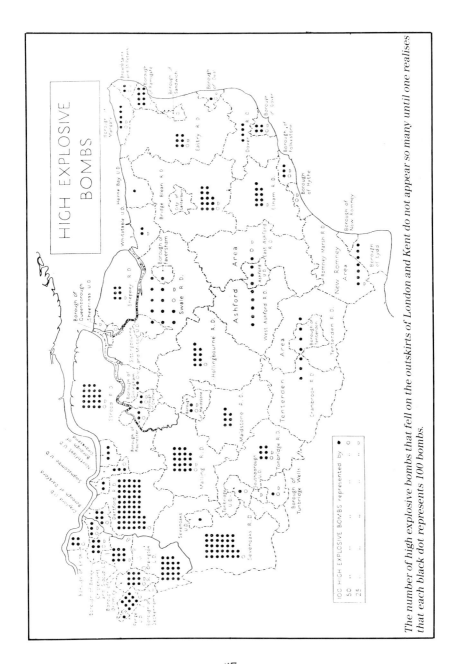

The number of high explosive bombs that fell on the outskirts of London and Kent do not appear so many until one realises that each black dot represents 100 bombs.

"BOMB ALLEY"—AND THE LOAD IT TOOK FROM LONDON

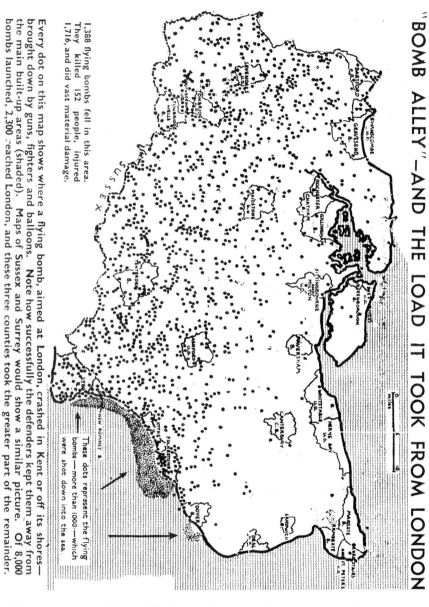

1,388 flying bombs fell in this area. They killed 152 people, injured 1,716, and did vast material damage.

Every dot on this map shows where a flying bomb, aimed at London, crashed in Kent or off its shores—brought down by guns, fighters and balloons. Note how successfully the defenders kept them away from the main built-up areas (shaded). Maps of Sussex and Surrey would show a similar picture. Of 8,000 bombs launched, 2,300 reached London, and these three counties took the greater part of the remainder.

These dots represent the flying bombs—more than 1000—which were shot down into the sea.

Kent was known as 'Bomb Alley' according to the diagram in the local Government Service Journal of 1944. The flying bombs V1's and V2's were all meant for London.

68

Down Faversham Way

by

D.C. JORDAN

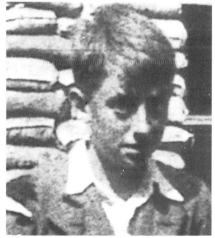

F-A-V-E-R-S-H-A-M we spelt out as the train slowed to a stop; passing the station nameboard as it did so. We had reached our unknown destination. This was no ordinary mystery tour though, but the final outcome of a Government Committee. "Evacuation in Wartime" had been the subject of the committee's investigation, and on October 27th 1938, its recommendations were accepted.

This was an exciting adventure, we were all 12 year olds. I was being "Evaporated"; complete with my gas mask, identity label and a knapsack of essential clothing. I was with my new school mates, having passed the examination for Chatham Junior Technical School earlier in 1939. We would be pupils for three years, and at the end, almost certainly become apprentices in H.M. Dockyard, Chatham.

We were marshalled as a group on the station platform and marched across the road to the Queen's Hall. Here we encountered Rev. C. Terence Spurling. I was fairly certain that we would have encountered a nurse who would be looking for defects or infestations! We were given a paper carrier bag (plastic had not been invented then) containing our "Iron Rations". This comprised a tin of corned beef, condensed milk, biscuits and some other bits. Our last task was to complete a pre-printed postcard with our new address on to send to our parents. They had no idea where we were going to end up.

Our parents lived in the Naval Dockyard towns of Chatham, Gillingham, and Rochester. They had to accept that they were in a "Military Target" area. It was felt certain that heavy air raids would cause many fatalities and devastate the area. It was against this background they had said "Goodbye" to their children, posssibly for the last time.

We were ready to set off to meet our new "Aunties" and "Uncles". Kind-hearted Faversham folk had opened their doors to these likely orphans from the Medway Towns. I found myself billeted with an older "Second-year" from Chatham Junior Technical School. I expect he was asked to keep an eye on me. We were billeted with Mr. and Mrs. Parnell at their home in Ospringe Road.

We came to be in an Air Raid Shelter when the air raid warning sirens sounded, soon after war was declared at 11 am on Sunday, September 3, 1939. I was half way up the escape ladder at the back when the Air Raid Warden came down the front steps of the house. I thought we would be told off. We were – for not having our gas masks with us! There was a war on and he had plenty on his mind besides worrying about us.

But what air raid?

It was the first of many false alarms. What we did not know was a very early form of Radar was already in operation. The signals picked up were not always what they seemed and the operators lacked experience.

The four tall metal masts so clearly visible on Boughton Hill from Faversham were part of this "Radio Direction Finding" (R.D.F.) system. Nobody knew this at the time and all the boys were quite certain that they sent "Death Rays" upwards to kill enemy pilots. Others were equally sure that "Magnetic Beams" were emitted to stop the engines of enemy planes. Why, everyone knew of cars or lorries that had suddenly stopped when testing was going on!

Little did we realise that in the following year R.D.F. would play such a big part in the "Battle of Britain".

It was still holiday time for schoolboys despite the war. We had much free time to find our way about our new town. Even so we had to report to various spots at given times for our teachers to "count heads". One such place was The Mount. Someone organised us into sand-bag filling teams. These were used to protect essential buildings, such as the cottage hospital in Stone Street, the police station and the fire station from bomb blast damage. On the principle that one boy does half a man's work and two boys together produce nothing but chaos, I'm not sure how a gang of boys and a heap of sand got on together!

Hop picking time came along but I am not sure if the Londoners came that year. I went with my companion and Mrs. Parnell to the hop gardens in the London Road (opposite St. Ann's Road). It was not my most favourite pastime, and Mrs. Parnell would yell "Pick" every time I found something more interesting to do. I never missed food time though!

The effect of the war on rail transport is rarely mentioned but I suspect that in the early days of the war, some disorganisation was experienced. This may have explained the glut of fruit in Faversham. We evacuees were given apples and plums which we had to go and collect from various farms.

Eventually, school work had to start. How our teachers had managed to arrange accommodation for the nine classes making up the three years of Chatham Technical School I do not know. Whilst we operated as a complete group we were scattered in rooms in schools, halls and the library. Mainly we used the Wreight School, next to St. Mary's Church and St. Ann's School in St. Ann's Road. It must have been a little chaotic, but to us it seemed to be something to be expected from "grown ups". Our main assembly as a whole unit for the week was at morning service at St. Mary's Church. We had classes all day on Saturdays (it was usual to have Saturday morning classes in those times) and I suspect that we had time off in the week.

By November, things had got into a routine. The "Phoney War" did not seem to be doing much and our main concern was "The Black Out". "Put that light out," would ring out if a passing Air Raid Warden spotted a chink of light. I have not seen such starry nights since though and it is amazing how our modern street lighting seems to have robbed us of this incredible sight. Moonlit nights came to be feared as the war progressed.

During this month I received a message that my mother was in hospital and arrangements were made for me to catch the No. 26 bus home. This ran from Faversham to Gravesend regularly. Children under 14 were not allowed to visit patients then, so my father bought my first pair of long trousers, so that I "looked the part". Schoolboys in short trousers were the norm in 1939. My mother had a gall bladder operation, a serious thing then. The wards seemed so crowded, but of course space was being kept for the expected air raid casualities.

I returned to Faversham and to school with a heavy heart, but at least with long trousers! I was on the road to being "grown up".

My mother recovered, but was not well enough to have me home at Christmas as did other parents. So it was Christmas away for me. It was a white christmas, and in fact the start of one of the coldest winters of the century (an official secret then). We enjoyed the snow and ice but I always felt cold. With our insulated attics, double glazing and central heating now, it is difficult to realise how cold it could be indoors then. The water pipes froze in Ospringe Road, and I recall getting buckets of water from a nearby bake-house. The smell of fresh bread and the warmth there lingers still; as does the song "Somewhere over the Rainbow," very popular at the time. It still makes me feel homesick.

This song came from the film "The Wizard of Oz" which we saw at the Odeon or Embassy cinemas as they were then called. "Going to the pictures" was the social event and we boys were keen film fans. Col. Neame (of Shepherd and Neame the brewers) showed us a coloured film of his big game hunting in Africa. This must have been at Rev. Spurling's club at the Queens Hall. Some of our school mates were billeted at Syndale House, the home of Col. Neame, and told us tales of being waited on by servants. How true this was I do not know, but there were still many young women "in service" in those days.

After the cold winter a type of flu seemed to strike the school children. My mother, now fully recovered came to collect me when she heard that I was ill. On my return to Faversham, following my recovery, I found myself in a new billet, with Mr. and Mrs. Brown of St. Marys Road. They had a son of my age, with the same christian name. I cannot remember how we got over the confusion this must have caused. We got on well together and I was able to have my bicycle sent by train. This extended my range around the local countryside.

Together we rode the lanes which were free of motor traffic, due to the petrol shortage (and the fact that few cars were then about).

Seasalter was within our reach via Goodnestone and Graveney, a run out that has changed little over the years. Along the Swale and in the Thames estuary sailing barges were such everyday things that we hardly gave them a second look. As far as we were concerned they had been there for ever, and would remain so. Similarly, the horses used for farm work were a common sight, along with carts. Where the M2 runs over the valley there used to be a lake. The trip included a ride through the then flooded Water Lane at Ospringe. At this lake a ewe gave birth to a lamb giving me an insight to "the facts of life", a subject not much gone into then. We also came across a drowned lamb there.

"We're Going to Hang Out the Washing on the Siegfried Line" we used to sing. The German front line was so named and the French had the Maginot Line opposite. The Germans outflanked this by invading Belgium and the Netherlands in May 1940. I remember little of this, but we did discover soldiers putting up barbed wire barriers at Seasalter beach. This prevented us from getting cockles and winkles there. We were most put out about this. In addition, German paratroops had been dropped in the Low Countries in civilian clothes complete with bicycles, so we found ourselves faced by armed men on our trips out at times. These were ours, I hasten to add.

The Medway Towns were never seriously bombed and it was quite unforeseen that Canterbury would be blasted in the way it was.

At the start of the war there was the Auxiliary Fire Service. This comprised of volunteers who were equipped with "trailer pumps". One of our sources of interest was to watch them practise with long stretches of hoses, their pumps sucking water out of The Creek and squirting it back in again. A typical "grown-up" sort of trick we concluded.

There are memories too of standing on the long footbridge from the Recreation Ground to Preston to watch the steam engines manoeuvre the trucks in the goods yard. One engine numbered 1066 was driven by William the Conquerer we decided.

Clearly, Faversham was not going to be such a good place for evacuees and eventually, a decision was taken for our re-evacuation to South Wales. As far as Chatham Technical School was concerned, this meant going to Pontypridd in the Rhonda Valley, somewhat different to Faversham. The eight months, we had spent in Faversham seemed more like eight years to us at that age.

Denis Jordan moved to Deeping St. James near Peterborough when he retired from working at Chatham Dockyard following its closure in 1983. He is married with two sons and two grandchildren.

Summer in the Country
by
CAREY BLYTON

I LAY on my mother's bed by her side and, as the engine of the V1 cut out, held my breath, waiting for the explosion. When it came, it was as though the end of the world had come. The house shuddered and the room filled with dust and flying glass; the noise was deafening. It was a warm July night in 1944, and the time was 9 pm.

The doodlebug had fallen on the last house but one in a terrace of eight houses diametrically opposite ours. The memories of that night are, even after 45 years, still vivid and powerful although, like a broken kaleidoscope, they are made up of jagged fragments which no longer fit together in any semblance of order or pattern.

I was 12 years old. My father, an Air Raid Warden, was on duty and so not in the house at the time. My sister was out playing tennis. My first clear memory was of somehow making my way upstairs to the toilet through broken glass, broken tiles, plaster, household items – many in bizarre twisted shapes – and the acrid smell of cordite. I saw the Vicar picking his way precariously up the stairs through the debris. He asked me if I was alright. I was, but I was very worried about our cat. He said he would look for the cat. He disappeared downstairs again, crunching over the broken glass and tiles.

The door of the toilet was no longer on its hinges but halfway down the narrow landing, locked in a kind of insane embrace with the door of my own bedroom, the two inextricably jammed together by the force of the blast. They were leaning crazily against a bookcase on the landing. I could hear running water to my right, in the bathroom next door.

Later, I managed to get into the various bedrooms and was fascinated by the mad chaos I found in them: the contents of drawers and wardrobes all over each room, broken mirrors, smashed furniture and plaster, glass and tiles underfoot. Most bizarre of all, in the front bedroom, there were great bulging 'sacks' of shattered glass where the window panes had broken and all the pieces were held in by the wire-mesh of the protecting frames, which had stretched but not broken. Splinters of glass, some as long as kitchen knives, were embedded in the doors of the wardrobe in my father's room. In my sister's room at the back of the house, some of the coiled, spiral net-curtain wires had stretched out with the blast; one was still attached to the window frame at one end but with its other end embedded in the wall opposite, the wire stretched across the room as taut as a telephone wire.

I recall wandering about in a kind of daze, not really aware of the fact that the street was now full of people: air raid wardens, police, ambulancemen, firemen, neighbours. My sister arrived, looking incongruous in her tennis gear.

I went back downstairs and into the sitting room which had become my mother's bedroom some time before, as her ever-worsening rheumatoid arthritis made it impossible for her to get upstairs. By this time, my father had arrived and I was aware that he was endeavouring to make some sort of arrangement on the telephone – miraculously still working – with an aunt who lived at Eltham, so that my mother and I would have somewhere to go. Clearly, with every pane of glass in the house gone and virtually every tile stripped from the roof by the blast, we could not stay in the house for the night.

It was at this point that it dawned on me just how lucky my mother and I had been. We were shocked and bruised but otherwise unharmed. My right shin was hurting where, as I lay on my mother's bed, an art deco lightshade – a large, thin copper ring with a fringe of minute beads – had fallen on it, its flex severed by a piece of flying glass. On the other side of the french windows of my mother's room was a glass conservatory, now entirely denuded of glass, including the glass roof. Incredibly, all the glass had been sucked into the garden by the blast, rather than being blown into the room. I felt quite sick as I thought of the many glass 'daggers' imbedded in the furniture in the front bedroom upstairs. My own bedroom, the little boxroom over the front door, was next to it, and I might well have been in it. I was glad that I had been downstairs, lying on my mother's bed: this was so as to be near the reinforced stair-cupboard, which we all used as a shelter during air raids.

The real damage, to my hearing, did not become apparent until the 1960s, when tinnitus was finally confirmed by tests in 1970. At the time, the ringing in my ears, caused by such a close explosion, died down and all seemed to be well.

My father told us that we were to go to my aunt's house at Eltham, and that he would take us in the car. We helped my mother with her two walking-sticks down the hall, through the front door and down the front path to the kerbside to await the car. This was a slow and painstaking business, with so much debris underfoot. While waiting for the car at the kerbside I was able to see the appalling devastation the V1 had caused. Most of the house which it had struck was missing. The houses either side were very badly damaged. The road and the pavements were almost completely obliterated by broken glass, shattered tiles, odd items of clothing, household objects like saucepans and cutlery, smashed fence palings and so on.

There seemed to be an enormous number of people scurrying about, helping others and organising things. Someone I asked – whether a neighbour or an 'official' I do not now recall – told me that a lady in the house obliquely opposite to that house had been injured. The most extraordinary sight of that extraordinary night was a bath in the middle of the road. I was told that someone had been having a bath when the V1 dropped, and they ended up in the road; still in the bath, bruised but otherwise unhurt. There was no water in the bath.

"Hardly surprising," the man added with a grim laugh. Blast played such strange tricks frequently.

It was some time later I heard that a schoolfriend, who lived opposite the house which the V1 had struck had also been hurt. He had ignored his parents' pleas to come into the Morrison shelter with them when they heard the engine of the V1 cut out, and he had gone to the window to see where it landed. Since it landed about 40 feet in front of his face, he had been lucky not to have been killed. As it was, he had to have an emergency operation to remove a piece of shrapnel which had entered his brain through the forehead. He recovered from this without any after effects.

We finally set off on a journey from Beckenham to Eltham that went through a nightmare nocturnal landscape painted by Hieronymous Bosch. The night-sky was criss-crossed by searchlight beams, and the car jolted and shuddered through debris in the road a great deal of the time. The journey was also punctuated by occasional explosions, some near, some far off, as other V1's landed. I do not recall now, but we no doubt arrived on the rims of the wheels, since it must have been impossible to drive through so much broken glass without punctures.

When we arrived at Eltham we found that my aunt had made up two beds, one on the ground floor for my mother. We settled in for the night after a very welcome hot drink and, somehow or other, I managed to get to sleep. My last thought was not of my cat but of my white mouse, now a splendid vermilion colour. My bedroom had also been my laboratory. On going into it on my investigation of the damage upstairs, I had seen that a bottle of haemotylin – which I used to stain botanical specimens in my microscopy – had somehow been overturned by the blast and emptied itself out onto the marble top of a wash-stand I used for my chemical experiments. The mouse, having escaped its cage, was scampering madly through the spilled dye in its panic. I never saw this mouse again, though no doubt it gave the cat quite a surprise when it finally returned to the house.

My mother and I spent several days at Eltham. Meanwhile, my father tried to find us somewhere safe in the country and endeavoured to make all the necessary arrangements to have our house made secure from the weather and looters. I didn't see our house again until the autumn, by which time it had been re-tiled – twice – and much of the damage of that dreadful night had been put right. My father was not very happy about the itinerant Irish labour force that the Government was using to make good this sort of war damage. Many things "went missing" and my father was often to say, later on: "I'm not sure which was worse – what Hitler did to our house or what the Irish did while repairing it". Certainly, some very nice things vanished without a trace, but looting immediately after bombing was not unknown, so it would be pointless to attempt to apportion blame. It was just a fact of life then, part and parcel of the total disruption of life that occurred to many.

After a few days, my father was able to arrange for my mother and me to be taken as evacuees at a rectory in Somerset; so we packed our few belongings and awaited the transport one bright, sunny morning.

Being a Cockney from Bermondsey, my mother got along well with the two ambulancemen who drove us down to West Lydford in Somerset. They were very kind and solicitous, while full of typical London 'blitz' humour: my mother gave them as good as she got. But it was a very hot day and the journey seemed to me to be endless. Out of thought for my mother's comfort and because, at the beginning, the roads around London, with all their debris, did not allow for speeding, they drove fairly slowly. So we cooked in the hot sun, cooped up in the ambulance.

Finally, at about 5 pm, we arrived, and it was to prove to be the start of two very extraordinary months – probably the most extraordinary of my life.

As the ambulance turned off the road onto the short gravel drive leading up to the front of the house I noticed two things. There had clearly once been iron gates, now missing and presumably surrendered to the war effort. Close to the entrance of this drive, the road went over a river by means of a brickwork bridge.

The ambulance came to a stop at the front door or entrance porch of what seemed to me to be a house of immense size. In front of this was a lawn, running down to a river, on which was an enormous tree which I later discovered was a ginkgo or maiden-hair tree.

The Rector's wife came out to meet us and, after introductions were made, led the way to a large, ground floor room overlooking the front lawn that was to be my mother's bedroom. Having helped my mother to her new quarters, the ambulancemen, anxious to get back to London, refused tea politely and took their leave. My mother and I thanked them for their help. We took tea with the Rector's wife and then I was shown to my room, one of very many upstairs, close to the rooms occupied by the two children of the house. These were two boys, named Rene and Francois; the Rector's wife was French.

The Rectory was a large, rambling house of some twenty rooms, set in grounds of several acres. The River Brue bordered the large lawn at the front of the house. As I looked out from the portico, to the left, there were fields and rough pastures. At the back of the house there were stables and barns and many other out-houses of various sizes. I discovered, many years later, that the foundations of the house were Elizabethan, but there had been many successive additions and alterations so that it was, architecturally, a muddle of Georgian and Victorian styles. The portico was Georgian, with several pillars, and the large kitchen area was floored with huge, irregular stone 'pavings'. My mother's room was large, with french windows which gave a fine view of the front lawn and the enormous ginkgo tree. My own room, upstairs, was much smaller. Its little window looked out at the back of the house onto a sort of courtyard and onto stables and out-houses. In the first few days I explored the house and the grounds. I was full of wonder that anyone could live in what seemed to me to be such grandeur and in such quiet and solitude that the war, so far away in and around London, might have been on another planet.

As July turned into August I settled in, although my mother was finding it hard to adjust. For her, the change and the differences seemed a little too much. Even I, at 12 years old, realised that she was not at all happy. The main problem was the Rector's wife, who was a hard woman, very different from her husband, a quiet and gentle Welshman, completely dominated by her. We had not been there very long before there was a row between my mother and the Rector's wife concerning "the fall of France". I never knew the details but I gathered that the British Expeditionary Force was accused of "deserting its allies".

I realised later on that what upset my mother most of all was the fact that if there was any trouble with the "the boys" – Rene, Francois and myself – then it was always I who was blamed. My mother refused to believe the Rector's wife when she said I was a "bad influence" and retaliated, as politely as she could, that Rene and Francois seemed to her to be spoiled; which they were.

But I was too involved in exploring the house and the grounds to be very much aware – or even concerned – about my mother. I had always throughout my childhood shown a great interest in natural history, so I was now in my element. At the rear of my own garden in Beckenham was a wood of a few acres through which ran the River Beck. But it was a small stream and I had never caught anything other than sticklebacks and the occasional gudgeon or roach washed down from the lakes at Kelsey Park, a mile or two upstream, after flooding from heavy rain. So the River Brue was a magnet to which I was drawn throughout my time at West Lydford.

It had everything for me. Where it bordered the grounds of The Rectory it was slow-moving and quite deep – some four or five feet, with occasional parts a little over six feet. There were many water lilies and other water plants and weeds, and it was also the part where the Rector's wife and we boys swam. I can still feel the extraordinary sensation in my legs as dozens of minnows attempted to eat the hairs, made erect by the cold water as I descended the wooden ladder attached to the bank.

It was here at the River Brue that I developed a healthy respect for water. Before, attending the local swimming baths in Beckenham, I did not think too much about any possible dangers. But at West Lydford something occurred which made me much more aware. Being a little impatient to get out of the river after swimming, the ladder being occupied by both the Rector's children, I attempted to get out straight onto the bank. The top of the bank was about two feet above the water level, so I grabbed the grass at the top and started to heave myself up. I did not know, of course, that there was a bend in the river at this point, and that the bank was deeply undercut. My legs suddenly went under the bank and, the more I struggled, the further they went, my hands slipping down the slope of the bank. Most of my body seemed to be disappearing underneath the bank and my head was starting to go under. I screamed with fright and the Rector's wife, seeing at once what was wrong, seized my wrists and managed to pull me up onto the bank, where I lay gasping and shivering with fear. Instead of comforting me she gave me a short lecture on the sin of impatience, and told me to wait for the ladder in future. "That's why it's there," she added. "It's too dangerous to try and get out onto the bank straight from the water – the bank is undercut all the way along here".

But the nature of the river changed dramatically once it reappeared after passing under the road at the road bridge. There was a very small weir or lock gate there so that the water fell into a large pool and then ran much faster and much shallower in and out of pools of slower water under willow trees.

Before the bridge, the river seemed to contain mostly minnows and eels in enormous numbers, with a few perch. But below the bridge, where the water splashed and gurgled over stones and in and out of the little pools of slower water, there were chub and trout, the former often reaching one to two pounds, in weight, dace, roach and gudgeon. There was even the smaller type of perch known as the Miller's Thumb or Bullhead.

Fortunately I had brought my rod and tackle with me, so straight away my days were spent fishing, from the moment I left the breakfast table until it was time for bed. It was at West Lydford that I caught my very first trout, though not in a way to gladden the heart of a game-fisherman...

It was at The Rectory at West Lydford that my interest in natural history really began to mature, for in that hot summer of 1944 I discovered for myself so many of the mysteries of nature that I had only read about. I already had many books on natural history, including quite a number that had belonged to my paternal grandfather, Thomas Carey Blyton, the father of the children's writer, Enid Blyton. It was he who had taught my aunt her love of nature and how to identify wild animals and wild flowers.

One of my favourite books at this time was in fact one of my grandfather's books, "The Natural History of Selbourne" by the Rev. Gilbert White. Sadly, this was one of the many things which "went missing" at the time we were away from the house because of the V1. I have always regretted this very much, as my grandfather had water-coloured most beautifully all the black and white illustrations in the book, according to the natural colours of the birds and animals.

I discovered the chrysalises of moths and butterflies in the vegetation bordering the river and, keeping them in jars in one of the stables, was able to observe these delicate and graceful creatures hatching out. I was very excited when a small batch of pale lemon-coloured chrysalises hatched out into lacewings – beautiful, fragile creatures with lace-like wings the colour of mint jelly.

I spent many a happy hour crouched down in the faster moving parts of the river, my bottom oblivious to the water, lifting up stones and examining the many and varied creatures that lived under them: caddis larvae, water shrimps, leeches, water scorpions and even, on one occasion, a small crayfish. My first face-to-face encounter with a Miller's Thumb, one of nature's most horrendously ugly creations with its broad, squat face and spiny fins, gave me quite a scare. Looking back, I expect it was more scared than I was since it shot away and was gone in an instant.

I was able to watch the many bats which came out in the dusk, flitting silently across the surface of the river and, from the windows of my bedroom, emerging from under the eaves of the roof. One night a bat came into my room and although it was very late I rushed down to my mother's room to tell her all about it, in great excitement. But she seemed to be more concerned that I had not brought it down with me.

I was intrigued by the many molehills in the rough pastures and fields to the side of the house, never having seen such things before but, although I spent much time in still, silent watchfulness, I was never able to see a mole.

However, I did see a barn owl – at very close quarters. In one of the fields were the remains of a stone-built barn or out-house. I investigated this very early on in my stay at The Rectory. Only two walls were still standing, at right angles to one another, and the roof had vanished, leaving only a few rafters. As I entered this ruin for the first time and looked around, a barn owl, obviously resting up during the day in a niche close to my head, suddenly took flight in alarm. It was so close to me that its wing brushed my face, giving me quite a fright. It abandoned the ruin after this for I never saw it again, although I did see an owl make a kill one evening in one of the fields nearby.

It was at West Lydford that I saw my first fieldmice and my first slow-worm, and, near the end of my stay there, lizards basking in the warm afternoon sun, lying on top of the brickwork of the bridge over the river.

And it was at The Rectory that I first discovered mason bees. These lived in holes in the crumbling mortar of one of the stables and I was totally fascinated by them. I developed a way of studying them better by fixing a jam jar over a mason bee hole with plasticene and then, when it emerged, whipping the jar off and quickly putting it down on the ground inverted. These bees were quite small and appeared to live alone. I never gave them a chance to prove whether or not they could sting.

In one of the out-houses, among all the bric-a-brac, I found a very old gin trap hanging up on a rusty nail. In "demonstrating" how this ghastly mechanism worked Francois managed to get his foot caught in it. Fortunately it was a very old trap, as well as rusty, and the spring had lost much of its power. This incident caused a great furore and – hardly surprisingly – I was held to be responsible for Francois' "terrible wound". This appeared to be very slight damage to his shoe, as far as I could see. Naturally, I was banned from going into the out-houses after this, although allowed to continue to use the stable with my ever-growing collection of specimens in jam jars.

It was at West Lydford that I managed, for the first time, to catch fish using an artificial fly, which I did in the pool below the weir. But I did not have the patience to do this more than a few times and soon reverted to the more usual – and very much quicker – method of either worm or grasshopper, caught in the grass verges at the side of the pool.

It was while fishing the pool from the bridge that I first met a remarkable man, who was to teach me a great deal about the river and its ways. Above all, how to fish it. His name was Mr. Richards and he was in an old-fashioned, self-propelled wheelchair, the kind that had a sort of bicycle pedal mechanism at the front with two handles for turning. The way he was able to manoeuvre this contraption around on the slopes of the river bank was quite extraordinary. It took me a little while before I was able to accept the fact that it was not going to run away with him and tip him headlong into the river. He must have had extremely strong arms and shoulders. I never saw his legs as these were covered with some sort of oilskin which buttoned or press-studded all over the chair.

When I asked at The Rectory about him I was told that he had "trench feet" which he had got in the Great War, and that he had been in a wheelchair ever since. I had no idea what "trench feet" were and at the time, imagined they were the remains of feet that had been gnawed away by rats. It was some years before I learned that "trench feet" were feet that had been severely frost-bitten.

However, his disability did not stop him from fishing, which he did most of the time, and it was Mr. Richards who gave me advice about how to fish the river. I soon learned that the fishing of the deeper, slow-moving part of the river above the bridge was quite different from the fishing of the faster, shallower water below it. By the time I met Mr. Richards I had all but abandoned the upper river, having quickly tired of so many eels and, when one raised the bait off the bottom, the incessant pestering of minnows. He taught me how to catch the perch there by fishing very shallow but very large baits, too big for the minnows to get their mouths around. So it was either an enormous lug worm or – poetic justice perhaps – a minnow itself used as a bait for perch.

It was he who first told me about grasshoppers for chubb bait: "you don't need bread or maggots or whatever – all the bait you need is around you, all about the river". The Rector's wife welcomed this as it meant that I did not have to have pieces of meat hanging up rotting, with large flower-pots full of sawdust underneath to catch falling maggots.

He also told me about the big, fat juicy grubs that one could obtain from old cow pats, the ones the sun had dried out: chub found these irresistible, although the Rector's wife did not. She tried very hard to make my mother stop me from turning over the old cow pats for bait, saying it was "disgusting and most unhygienic". Once she realised that it was a practice that I would not give up she made me scrub my hands with a brush before every meal.

My mother and I had been at The Rectory about two weeks when two more "evacuees" arrived to stay there. Col. Trench, a retired military man, and his French wife added a certain interest, and now I heard a great deal of French spoken as the Rector's wife and Mrs. Trench talked endlessly. I have no doubt that my mother and I were discussed at length.

Col. Trench was a game-fisherman, and he was soon out and about fishing for trout in the river. But, unlike me, he used artificial flies. On one occasion I bagged a fine brace of trout which he admired with many congratulations. But as soon as he learned that I had caught them with *worms* his admiration evaporated and from that moment he became somewhat distant and aloof, keeping himself very much to himself. It was my first intimation of the snobbery associated with game-fishing.

However, I was not to change my ways and I continued to catch the occasional trout, which I always took back for my mother to eat, using worms or grasshoppers caught along the river-side. I really enjoyed the "stalking" – wriggling on my stomach through the long grass in a slow, careful approach to one of the pools by the willows and then carefully and slowly lowering the live bait into the water at the head of the pool and allowing the current to take it to the foot of the pool, where the chub and trout lay in wait. It was very rarely that a fish did not rise to it and even rarer that I did not catch something.

Although the Rector's wife was prepared to have the trout I caught cooked for my mother – and occasionally for me also – she and her family would never eat them. Possibly this was a form of protest; or maybe a way of showing that her allegiance lay with the Trenches, who were of her own class. My mother and I clearly were not. All this occurred to me much later on. At the time I was always sad that the beautiful irridescent colours of the rainbow trout disappeared in the cooking. The rainbow trout is probably the most beautiful fish to be found in our rivers, although the handsome perch, with its orange fins, is a strong contender.

Another "new face" appeared one day while I was fishing in one of the pools below the bridge. A young, swarthy man appeared right beside me. It gave me a shock as I had not heard his approach, as I was intent on what I was doing. To my amazement he was carrying a bow and had a quiverful of arrows on his back. For a moment I wondered if it was Pan, but he turned out to be otherwise.

He was a very taciturn individual, answering my many questions with monosyllables. He told me his name was Protheroe which, for a long time, I assumed was his Christian name and that he was a "traveller". This meant nothing to me at the time. When I showed him that I was after trout, using worms, he said: "That's a lot of hard work. I'll show you a quicker way than that". He then moved slowly and carefully down to a lower pool where there was a small copse of trees. He stood in their shelter for a little while, studying the water. Then, again slowly and carefully, he fitted an arrow into the bow and drew it back. He aimed for quite a long time, the muscles in his forearm standing out under the strain. Then he released the arrow. It entered the water with a hiss and – to my astonishment – a large trout came up to the surface, threshing about, transfixed by the arrow. Protheroe waded into the water and picked it up. He removed the fish from the arrow and slipped it into a bag at his waist, returning the arrow to the quiver.

I was terribly excited and almost speechless. I finally found my tongue and asked him a dozen questions, but he just smiled and said: "Like I said. It's a lot quicker". He turned and walked off, and I ran back to The Rectory to tell my mother all about this extraordinary event. I am not sure if she fully believed me since I was known to be a "highly imaginative child". But, whether she believed me or not, she listened patiently to all that I poured out in my excitement. "Well, well" was all she could say, over and over again.

I was to see Protheroe a few more times before we left The Rectory, but never again did I see him with his bow and arrows. It was many years before I realised that catching fish with a bow was probably just a sideline for him: his main quarry must have been rabbits. An arrow is a lot quicker than setting snares and then returning to them later – and not likely to alert a farmer of Protheroe's presence. I suppose he was possibly the most unusual poacher I could ever have met.

Now that Mr. Richards had given me advice about the upper part of the river I varied my fishing between the little pools below the bridge and the slower, deeper water above it. It was in fact the very first time I tried the latter, fishing from the road bridge, that I caught an eel. This was a great excitement for me, being the first eel I had ever caught. I watched in a kind of horrified stupor as it twisted itself into knots on the end of the line, the slime from its body – thick and jelly-like – getting all over the line, the brickwork of the bridge and my hands as I vainly tried to disentangle it and remove the hook. This proved to be an impossible task and after a while the tightly, knotted and contorted mass fell off the line and back into the river. The eel had simply bitten through the line.

I remembered that one needed special hooks for eels, so I went straight back to The Rectory and wrote a letter to my father telling him all about this adventure and asking him to send me some eel hooks. I posted the letter at once. It did not occur to me at the time that my father had quite enough on his plate, what with the house to be made habitable again, worrying letters from my mother about her unhappiness at The Rectory and his concerns over his business. He had in fact "lost" several premises in the City in quick succession through incendiary bombs. It says much about my father that I received a reply return of post enclosing a packet of special eel hooks. He was like that.

I was so happy exploring the river and the surrounding countryside that I was quite oblivious of the fact that my mother was becoming more and more unhappy at The Rectory. Looking back, I realise that it was not really any one thing that caused her such distress but a whole catalogue of things which added up to a decision on her part to get away as soon as possible.

But I was aware of the awkwardness at the dining-table. My mother and I would sit at one end with our rations: the 2 ounces of butter per week and the other minute quantities of this and that. The Rector and his family sat at the other end and they had plenty of everything. There were all kinds of home-made jams and similar "country fare". We were never offered any of it. My mother had the generous heart of the Cockney – "share and share alike". The "them and us" attitude must have been incomprehensible to her, especially in the house of a man of the cloth.

On one occasion, I found my mother crying in her room. When I asked her why, she was at first reluctant to tell me, but when I pressed her she told me that the Rector's wife had all but shouted at her that she had "given in" to her illness. She included, for good measure, that she did not really need two walking-sticks to walk with, and, if she put her mind to it, she could walk quite well without them. I was horrified. I had seen my mother fight her appalling illness every inch of the way, ever since I could remember. It had begun as a complication from puerperal fever at my birth in 1932. It was at this point, I think, that I realised we could not stay at The Rectory. My mother said she would write to my father and ask him to find us alternative accommodation.

Then something occurred which may possibly have accelerated our departure. I got drunk. I occasionally borrowed a rather large lady's bicycle from The Rectory on which to cycle into the nearest town, Shepton Mallet. On this particular occasion, as I returned from the town, I stopped off to watch the men cutting the corn in one of the fields adjacent to the road.

It was a very hot day and the men offered me a drink of the strong, rough cider of Somerset. I do not, to this day, know how much of it I drank. Finally, realising that time was getting on and I ought to be getting back to The Rectory, I endeavoured to mount the bicycle – and immediately fell off. The men helped me to remount and gave me a push. What followed was a bizarre bicycle ride, most of the details of which remain obscure to this day. I must have fallen off the bicycle into the ditch many times. When I finally arrived at The Rectory I was in a terrible state, grazed and bleeding in many places, with torn clothing and – worst of all – smelling like a brewery. It was just my misfortune that the very person I met upon my arrival was the Rector's wife who, after a fit of the vapours and near-hysteria, dragged me off to my mother's room with loud exclamations of "Drunken little beast!" and "What can we expect from Londoners?" I must have passed out on my mother's bed, for I remembered nothing more until the evening. I was able to get cleaned up and make a fragile appearance in the dining-room for the evening meal. This was passed in glacial silence – apart from the colossal thumping in my head.

We had been at The Rectory almost one month. It was mid-August. I continued to enjoy the river and the countryside even more, for I knew that at any time these wonderful things would come to an end, perhaps for good. I threw myself into exploring and enjoying everything.

When the month was almost over my father appeared and told us that he had been able to find us alternative accommodation at the little country town of Castle Cary. This was a few miles away. He said we would be leaving The Rectory in a day or two, just as soon as he was able to arrange an ambulance for my mother.

I had mixed feelings about the announcement. I was sad at the thought of leaving such a beautiful and exciting place, but I was worried about my mother. Since the "drunken orgy", relations between ourselves and the Rector's family had been very strained. I knew my mother was anxious to get away. But I was intrigued by the name "Castle Cary" and its similarity to my own Christian name. I felt it was a good omen.

And, as so often happens, I made an exciting discovery too late to be able to take real advantage of it. On the other side of the road from the entrance to The Rectory drive was the opening of a lane which led to the church where the Rector took services. The lane ran parallel to the lower part of the river. Between it and the river was an immense hedge, some 12 to 14 feet high. While looking for moths and caterpillars one day, I discovered that one could actually enter the hedge. Within it, running the whole length of it for some hundred yards or so, was a sort of tunnel, the bottom of which was a dry ditch. This was an exciting discovery. When I walked down the "tunnel" I could see many birds' nests "from the inside. Not many of these were occupied so late in the year, although there was one which I was to study carefully. However, there was always such a commotion whenever I approached it "from the inside" that I took to passing it as quickly as possible for fear of frightening the parent birds into abandoning their young.

At last the day for our departure came. As the ambulance drove away from The Rectory I wondered what was in store for us. Had I known it at the time, it was to be very different from our time at The Rectory but happier for us both. But as the ambulance turned out of The Rectory drive, I watched the bridge and the river disappear from view with a heavy heart.

*Like his famous aunt Enid, **Carey Blyton** also become a writer. He has also followed a musical career and is a well known composer especially of television music. He now lives in Swanley, Kent with his wife and two grown up sons.*

The Rectory at West Lydford in which Carey Blyton spent the first part of his evacuation.

RECEPTION OF SCHOOL CHILDREN

FORM A

Instructions regarding Issue of Forms.

The form and counterfoil should be completed by the billeting officer in ink or indelible pencil except the space for the name of the Post Office at which payments will be made.

The full name and address of the occupier should be filled in.

The full name of each child should be filled in, a line being allowed for each child.   Any unused space should be cancelled.

The total number of children lodged at the premises should be filled in ; and the total amount payable per week to the occupier should be entered in words and not in figures.

The billeting officer should sign and date the form.

The counterfoil should be completed with all the particulars entered on the form.

The form should be handed to the occupier.   The counterfoils should be carefully preserved by the billeting officer.

Bureaucracy in World War II was no different from today.

92

Somewhere in France

19th February 1940

My Dearest Pat.

Thank you very much for your nice letter I am sorry I have not answered it before but I have such a lot to do I am sorry to hear Mummy has been unwell still I know you will be a good girl and look after her

How are you like having a new baby in the house, do you play with her or is she too young.

Well darling I will say goodnight & god bless you write to me soon

Your loving

Dad' x x x x x x x x x x
x x x x x x x x x

Pat Waller of Hoo received this letter from her father at Dunkirk shortly before he was evacuated. His father was among the first of Britain's armed forces to be sent abroad as he was already in the RAF, stationed at Hawkinge, when war broke out. The baby referred to in his letter was part of an evacuee family from London that Pat's mother looked after. Eventually they were moved to another house which was bombed and the whole family killed. Pat remembers her mother receiving a letter from Buckingham Palace signed by Queen Elizabeth the Queen Mother thanking her for helping to look after some of London's evacuees.

93

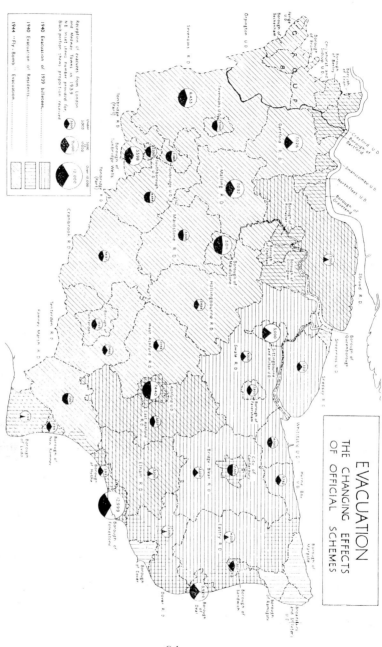

EVACUATION
THE CHANGING EFFECTS
OF OFFICIAL SCHEMES

Reception of evacuees from London
and Medway Towns in 1939.
The inset shows numbers provided for.
Black portion shows proportion received.

Under
1,000

1,000
7,000

Over
10,000

1940 Evacuation of 1939 billetees.

1940 Evacuation of Residents.

1944 - Fly-Bomb - Evacuation.

The 1945 map of Kent (which includes what is now part of London) shows not only how the original schemes over provided for evacuee numbers but also how the schemes adapted to changing circumstances.

94

The Entrepreneur
by
CAREY BLYTON

I REMEMBER little of the journey from West Lydford to Castle Cary except that it was quite short. Soon we were pulling up in front of a row of tiny terraced houses whose front doors opened straight out onto the pavement. This intrigued me as I had never seen houses like this before. Coming from a dormitory town where all the houses had front gardens, it was very strange.

A large, jolly woman was standing in the open doorway of the end house and she helped my mother and me carry our few belongings into the house. I felt like Alice after she had eaten the food to make her large – the house and its rooms seemed microscopic after The Rectory. The woman showed my mother into the tiny front room immediately to the right of the front door as we entered the house. There was a single bed in it and a single sash window which opened straight onto the street.

Once we had put our things down the large, jolly woman, whose name was Mrs. King, led us to the back of the house to a kitchen where we had tea. We passed another little room, the parlour, on the way.

In no time at all my mother and Mrs. King were getting on famously, Mrs. King "Tut! tut-ing!" over the things my mother was telling her about The Rectory and our time there. I was too overawed by the sudden change to say anything, as I drank my tea and looked around the tiny kitchen.

Suddenly I let out an exclamation, for I had seen through the little scullery window what appeared to be a gas holder in the garden! Mrs. King laughed. ".Why, bless me, of course it's a gas holder!" she said. "Mr. King is manager of the gas works and the house goes with the job." She took me outside at the back of the little house and across a small yard. There, in a large shed or open barn were several furnaces into which two men (stripped to the waist) were shovelling coal. I couldn't believe what I was seeing and stood there goggle-eyed like a hypnotised frog. I hardly noticed the two men as they said "Hello!" to me, being too engrossed at this extraordinary sight in someone's back yard. Mrs. King was highly amused by my reaction although, of course, she could not have known how different it was from The Rectory.

Mr. King turned up quite soon after, and Mrs. King introduced us to him. He was a small man with jet-black hair and, like his wife, was very friendly. We were given to understand that they had a daughter, Joan who was at work. We would meet her later when she came home.

My mother and I were made so welcome that we soon settled in. The contrast between the Rector and his family – landed gentry, I suppose one would call them – and the Kings who were working class, was considerable. While we were with them the Kings shared everything with us, whether it was a little something obtained "on the side" or something from a passing poacher. Mrs. King was kindness itself to my mother, and very tolerant of me, when, as I started to find my feet, became more 'stroppy'. Often, I was at a loss to know what to do with myself as the long, hot summer passed slowly.

I soon explored Castle Cary, its little High Street and other winding streets. I liked it very much. There seemed to be so much activity, so much "going on," compared with The Rectory and the timelessness of the river and the surrounding countryside. Then, one afternoon, something occurred that caused me a great deal of surprise and my mother a great deal of amusement.

It was a still August and the weather was hot, so my mother kept her sash window (with its wide sill) open most of the time. One afternoon I was in her room helping her put on her shoes when there appeared to be an eclipse of the sun. The room suddenly went very dark. Looking up, we saw an enormous bottom filling the open window. Its owner turned round and, in a slow, South American drawl, said: "Good day, ma'am". For a moment, neither my mother nor I could say anything. We just stared. I had never before seen a negro, that is, in the flesh, so I was not only stunned but also a little frightened. The owner of the enormous bottom was an enormous man. He was dressed in an American GI's uniform.

He introduced himself as "Joshua", adding "But my friends, they all call me Josh". My mother introduced us to him, and from that day on, Josh would often call in through the open window to say "Hello!" or sit on the sill and chat with my mother for a while. We discovered that a US Negro regiment was camped a few miles out of town at a place called Dimmer Camp. We did not know it at that time but the enormous massing of troops and equipment in the south of England, prior to the invasion of Europe, had already begun.

When Josh found out that my mother smoked he often gave her packets of American cigarettes – "Camel" or "Lucky Strike" – while I was given many a bar of "Babe Ruth" and similar American candies. He was always very generous and always laughing. I am sure he cheered my mother up a lot and she always looked forward to his almost daily visits.

Mrs. King didn't seem to mind that Josh – and on other occasions, Josh and one of his friends – sat on the window-sill chatting with my mother. "It helps pass the time, doesn't it? I mean, the poor lady can't get out and about much, can she?" she said. I couldn't help wondering what the Rector's wife would have said, in these circumstances.

The King's daughter, Joan, was as friendly and as kind as her parents. My mother and I were very quickly made to feel part of the family. I could even sense that my mother was a lot more relaxed now, so I was too.

At The Rectory there had been so much activity to fill my day that I was little trouble, appearing only at meal-times and for bed. The rest of the time I spent fishing or collecting specimens to put into the many jam jars and boxes which I kept in one of the old stables at the rear of the house.

97

At Castle Cary, however, time began to weigh a bit on my hands. There were few distractions to occupy me. So I began to be a bit of trouble, one way and the o' .er. One of the chemical experiments I conducted in the sink of Mrs. King's scullery resulted in my getting concentrated ammonia on one eye. I have the resultant damage to the cornea – "black spots in front of the eye" – to this day.

No doubt to avoid a repetition of such an occurrence Mrs. King suggested that I might like to help a friend and neighbour of hers who ran the little newsagent and sweet shop in the High Street. I agreed readily and, having been accepted as "suitable," spent several days helping out. But this did not last very long as I was caught "stock taking". My mother must have been very embarrassed but Mrs. King took this in her stride. After giving me a thorough box round the ears at my mother's insistence, all was forgiven, if not forgotten.

My next business venture was much more successful. Always interested in animals, I simply walked off the street into the waiting-room of the local vet and offered him my services. He was somewhat taken aback but, nevertheless, gave me a "job" washing out bottles and generally helping out at the back. I then dreamed up a scheme that was to be very rewarding financially for me. I soon realised that the vet had something of a problem in the disposal of the dead bodies of the pets he put down. I offered to dispose of them for sixpence a time. He accepted this offer readily. Terms concluded, I set about my business enterprise with a will!

I would place a dead cat, a dead dog (or whatever) on a wheel-barrow, trundle it round to the back of Mrs. King's and place it in one of the furnaces. The two men who worked at the little gas works were highly amused by this and were helpful with advice, although neither of them cared to push the body deep into the furnace with one of the long-handled rakes – I always had to do that. This macabre employment only once worried me. This was when the body of a Scots terrier was so swarming with fleas that it sounded like popcorn in the making as the body went into the furnace. The fleas exploded with the heat.

By now I was a popular fellow with Josh and his fellow GIs'. Enterprising as ever, I soon discovered that the Americans had a real passion for jewellery, no matter how cheap and garish. I had found a junk shop in Shepton Mallet and a similar sort of establishment in Castle Cary. In these two places I bought cheap, gimcrack jewellery with the money I earned from the vet's. I was also able to buy similar stuff at a chemist in Shepton Mallet. These were cheap rings, mostly, but I also bought chains for lockets and pendants.

These I bartered for American cigarettes. The cigarettes came in large packs of 200, 10 packets of 20; "Camel," "Lucky Strike," "Chesterfield" and so on. These exchanges were financially very much in my favour. The Americans were over-generous, giving whole packs of 200 cigarettes for small, cheap items of jewellery which had cost me very little. No doubt they paid very little themselves for the cigarettes as they were "Government issue" but, nonetheless, I did very well out of these barters. I sold packets of 20 cigarettes to all and sundry for one shilling each. I imagine that my mother's smoking rose considerably because of this cheap and ready supply.

However, like any intelligent "dope peddler," I refrained myself, content to make a handsome profit by selling to the addicted whilst abstaining. I did not start smoking myself until some six or seven years later, when I was about 18 or 19.

I cannot now recall if Mrs. King or Joan smoked but I was a regular supplier of cheap cigarettes to both Mr. King and the vet. In those days, smoking was very widespread. There was no lack of clients. My only concession to the trade, as it were, was to wear a particularly repulsive ring which I had acquired in a shop in Shepton Mallet: very large and vulgar but much admired by Josh. Several times he tried to make me part with it for larger quantities of cigarettes. But I always refused, much to my mother's amusement.

Looking back, those times must have been very strange for the inhabitants of Castle Cary, a quiet and sleepy little country town like many others in the West Country. Not only did they hear the slow, South American drawl in their streets, but also Italian.

There were quite a number of Italian prisoners of war in and around the town, helping local farmers harvest their crops. To me, they seemed rather a forlorn lot. They did not fit in with the mental image I had of the laughing, carefree Italians of Saturday morning cinema films. No doubt they were not simply homesick but also fed up with having to work the land in a foreign country. I don't suppose I would have been very happy if I had been an ex-waiter, having to hump sheaves of wheat about under a broiling sun. Or so I thought then, in my ignorance of real Italians. . .

Despite Government admonitions, a certain amount of fraternisation went on between these Italian POWs and the local inhabitants.

particularly the girls of course. I sometimes used to come across the odd couple, either talking in the street or, in the evening, walking arm-in-arm. On one occasion, when I was hunting butterflies in a field outside the town, I almost fell over a couple *in flagrante delicto.* I fled in haste; some of the Italians I had seen on my visits to Saturday morning cinema seemed to possess stilettos and carry on terrible vendettas. One evening I came across the King's daughter and an Italian POW in earnest conversation in a shop doorway. I don't suppose I would have thought any more about it but for a great upheaval which upset the even tenor of all our lives for a short time. Mr. King found out that his daughter was "carrying on" with an Italian POW.

I came into the little scullery one afternoon for tea, in the midst of what was obviously a great family row. Mrs. King was doing her kindly best to lower the temperature. I fled, with my heart thumping, but not before I heard Mr. King shouting: "Our young men aren't fighting the bloody Boche so you can carry on with some bloody Eyetie" – or words to that effect.

Things were very strained in the house for a few days but eventually they settled. I never again saw Joan with her Italian boyfriend. Whether that was because she had given him up, for fear of her father's anger, or because she was just much more discreet, I never knew. But the presence of the Italians certainly added a certain interest and colour to those times. I expect they left the odd bambino or two behind them when they finally departed.

My mother, who remembered all too well the bombs dropped on London by the Zeppelins in the Great War, was rabidly anti-German. Naturally she did not approve of any fraternisation with the Italian POWs who, she said "weren't that much better than the Huns, what with Mussolini using gas on the poor Abyssinians and all that".

If there was any trouble between the Italians and the American troops I was never aware of it. It's hard to believe there was any, since the negroes seemed to me to very easy-going and carefree men. But I was aware of the occasional hostility shown to the Americans by the local population, particularly in and around the local pubs where their pay, so much more than the British Tommies, allowed them to spend freely. But I saw only one fight involving a negro, although I never found out what it was all about. It was outside a pub called the "George Hotel" one evening. Possibly, locals had tried to prevent an American GI from spending his money in one of Castle Cary's "quality" pubs and the GI had tried to insist. My mother was shocked by what she saw as the local inhabitants' insensitivity, adding "and these poor boys, so far from their homes, are our allies, too".

My first real interest in music, which was to become my profession, began at Castle Cary. Prior to this, a naturally good treble voice had got me into the choir of St. George's, the parish church at Beckenham. I did not hold the position for very long owing to the sheer bloody-mindedness of the caretaker. We choirboys were paid sixpence for the two Sunday services and, after evensong one Sunday, I dropped my sixpence as we were all leaving the church. It rolled and dropped below the grating which ran all along the edges of the pews, either side of the central aisle. I was in the process of trying to get part of this grating up, in order to retrieve my money, when the caretaker insisted I left it and left the church forthwith. I did so, without my money, and I never went back into the church again. It was in fact many years before I would set foot in a church again since I equated the church with high-handedness and considered it a dishonest employer.

In the little parlour at the King's house was a piano. We had no piano at home and the only piano I had come across was that of a neighbour's in Beckenham. Then there was the school piano, which no-one was allowed to touch. So I had never actually *touched* the keys of a piano. At Castle Cary I was allowed free access to the King's piano and I spent a great deal of time picking out tunes with one finger. After a great deal of time and effort I was able to give a "recital" to my mother and Mrs. King. I regaled them with a complete – though "top part only" – rendition of Ivor Novello's "Keep the Home Fires Burning", a First World War song that had come into vogue again in the Second World War.

I was much encouraged in these efforts by both my mother and Mrs. King. After about a week, I was able to add to my repertoire other popular songs of the time, like "Lilli Marlene" and "Roll Me Over". "The Cornish Rhapsody", however, defeated me.

It is a sad but curious thing that, after returning to Beckenham in the autumn, my musical talent went into hibernation until I was convalescing from polio in 1947/48.

I was fascinated by the gas holder in the back yard of the King's house. It was not a very large one but, when full of gas, stood about 50 feet high. On its side was an iron ladder, firmly bolted to it. I had been warned by Mr. King to steer well clear of it altogether, right from the moment of our arrival. He explained to me how the holder operated using two glasses, one large and one small, the larger one set down on the table and the smaller one, inverted, representing the gas holder, going up and down inside it. He explained why there was water between the two, acting as a seal. He put the fear of God into me about the dangers of slipping off the ladder and falling between the two parts of the holder into the water. "If you were to come up *inside* the holder...," he added grimly. The smell of coal gas permeated the atmosphere all round the King's house and yard, so it acted as a constant reminder.

But of course, having been told so much only whetted my appetite. One day when the Kings were out visiting, I climbed up the ladder onto the top of the holder at a time when it was fully raised. It was a terribly exciting and exhilarating experience. I felt a tremendous sense of freedom. The wind blew my hair about and the views of the countryside around Castle Cary were spectacular. I spent quite a time up on the top, crossing over from one side to the other and clinging to the guard rail at the top, all around the perimeter, when near the edge. I was much more nervous when descending the ladder than when ascending it, fearful of slipping and ending up inside the holder.

I had visions of dying of coal gas poisoning. However, I regained *terra firma* without mishap.

I told no-one except my mother what I had done. She went white, and made me promise never to climb it again. I kept this promise since, once the adventure was over, I was in a terrible funk over what I had done. I was particularly worried about what would happen to us if Mr. King ever found out. One of the two men who worked at the furnaces must have been aware of my escapade since he made various sly remarks like "It's a nice day for taking in the view" and "It's 'King of the Castle' weather today," accompanied by heavy winks. But I never reacted and so never admitted anything.

And so the long, lazy summer passed and I filled my days with helping the vet "out at the back". Then there were the trips into Shepton Mallet and my well-paid "business ventures" involving cheap jewellery, and American cigarettes. My studies in natural history, so time-consuming at West Lydford, were replaced – without my realising it – by studies of my fellow men. I learned a lot in my month at Castle Cary about people's attitudes to one another; their attitudes to the war and to the impact of the war on their lives. My time at West Lydford had been time suspended, with all thoughts of the war banished. In Castle Cary I was constantly reminded of it by the sight of American army uniforms and the "POW" emblazoned on the clothing of the Italian prisoners of war.

The main V1 offensive lasted from June 6 to September 5, 1944, during which time just over 9,000 V1s were launched against the UK by the Germans. Although there were still more to come – some 1,500 in the period September 16, 1944 to March 29, 1945 – the worst of the onslaught was over by the first week of September, 1944. When this was realised, the return to London of the many children evacuated in June and July began.

My father reappeared, and I understood that our return to Beckenham was only a matter of days away. I viewed this with some regret, not least of all because it meant I would have to go back to school after so many weeks of absolute freedom. The prospect of sharing my lessons with the frogs in the flooded school shelters did not appeal to me – I preferred my natural history to be *al fresco*.

A day was fixed for an ambulance to take my mother and me back to Beckenham. The time had come to bid farewell to the many friends I had made in Castle Cary. These were Josh, the vet, the lady in the High Street newsagent and sweet shop, who had finally forgiven me for my "stock-taking," and many others. My suggestion that we telephoned the rector and his family in West Lydford, to say goodbye, was met with a mixture of amusement and irritation on the part of my mother. "No", she said firmly. "And anyway, we can't telephone – the Kings don't have a telephone". This settled the matter.

Finally, on yet another warm, sunny day, we took our leave of Castle Cary bidding the Kings a fond – and on my mother's part, tearful – farewell. As one might have expected, Mrs. King thoughtfully provided us with sandwiches and bottled stout for the journey.

As I watched the little streets of Castle Cary with their quaint shops and house facades disappearing from view I felt quite a wrench. My feelings were very mixed about the whole extraordinary summer. The two months, one at the rectory in West Lydford and the other at the house of the manager of the gas works in Castle Cary, could not have been more different. And yet, I would not have missed either month for anything. The first had given me my love of natural history; the second, my introduction to the world of music. These two strands in my make-up would be with me for life.

In August, 1980 whilst music tutoring for the Open University at the host University of Bath, it brought me to the West Country again, after a lapse of some 36 years. Although I knew it was foolish, I could not resist a return visit to both West Lydford and Castle Cary. Of course, one should never return to places that have been important to one, after a long lapse of time; it is better to remember them as they were. But I was unable to resist the temptation.

At West Lydford I discovered that The Rectory was now the private house of a local businessman who had men working for him "out at the back" in the various out-buildings. The house and grounds seemed little changed, although a sauna, set among the large, irregular stone 'pavings' on the ground-floor, appeared incongruous in a house whose foundations went back to Elizabethan times. And, as I expected, The Rectory seemed smaller than I recalled it.

More obvious changes were to be found in and around the river. The little lane from the road to the rector's church now sported a row of little houses and the enormous hedge had gone. Near the church was a narrow footbridge over the river. The river itself had been "modernised" – some of the grass verges I remembered of old were now cast in concrete. . .

Castle Cary seemed little changed, although the gas works had gone. There was nothing left of the furnaces and the giant shed that housed them. The gas holder itself had vanished. All that remained of it was a large, circular depression in the ground like some strange, neolithic remains. I rang the doorbell of "the manager's house" but there was no-one at home. So I contented myself with sitting on the window-sill, and peering into the little front room from the street. It was probably my imagination, but I thought I heard a slow, soft, South-American voice say: "Good day, ma'am".

*Like his famous aunt Enid, **Carey Blyton** also became a writer. He has also followed a musical career and is a well known composer especially of television music. He now lives in Swanley, Kent with his wife and two grown up sons.*

104

Memoirs of a War Baby
by
GRAHAM CLARKE

CHILDHOOD MEMORIES to be conjured up and set down in this way are odd things for all of us, but I suggest, especially for War Babies. For this war was at one and the same time the worst episode in the history of the whole world, but became absolute normality. It was a time, we realised later, of birth and early childhood, largely without our closest menfolk and almost ceaseless anxiety for the women left to cope.

Before the war my own father had been a bank clerk (more by necessity than inclination), but now he was away busy teaching the mysteries of wireless to fellow airmen in the RAF. This was a subject he understood well, it having been his hobby since his and its, early days. On several occasions he was informed that he was to be shipped overseas like so many other husbands and fathers; three times he bade us farewell with all its sadness and fears. In the event, our family were spared that ordeal and luckily he remained in England. He tried to visit us in the various secluded villages of our evacuation whenever he could, riding the length and breadth of Southern England on a great black iron bike.

As you would expect, the signposts and punctuation marks by which I chart my first few years, are in a vague order of chronology but are nontheless vivid and everlasting. The ghostly wailing of the Air Raid Siren; my first real orange, the deadly crump of a midnight bomb far too close. Of breaking my leg and seeing a mouse. A sudden smouldering gap in a familiar row of houses, the combined odour of burnt toast and paraffin and the worst one, of the Mickey Mouse Gas Mask. Also, the whispered neighbourly condolences over bereavement or about the price of margarine in the Home and Colonial Store.

Tempering the recalled realities are those notions and anecdotes supplied so liberally both at the time itself and subsequently over the teacups by aunts and grannies. Fathers, uncles and grandpas, of course, had their own stories to relate but they were of that other world of soldiers, sailors and airmen. Men, with the notable exception of one whom we were soon to meet, were in short supply. Aunts and grannies there were aplenty – not all actually related to us, of course (in fact my father's mother sadly died just before my birth), but others easily gathered during our times of retreat from newly suburban Hayes to our various places of evacuation. Hayes, in the London corner of Kent, is at the end of a railway line from Charing Cross, once a pretty country village itself; in the nineteen thirties it suddenly became a part of London, pleasant enough for a suburb but a suburb all the same. Hayes Common, however, with its acres of bracken, birch trees and mysterious earthworks, was close by and a little further was Caesars Wells and the magical Keston Ponds.

But these were only to be discovered and enjoyed later for there was a War going on. Mr. Adolf Hitler (a failed artist so we learn later) was the cause of all this commotion. A wicked and greedy man, he wanted to get England for himself and was determined to be nasty to our good and gentlemanly King George up in London. Hitler was a German (the words German and germ were absolutely synonymous for my first five years – one being merely the shortened form of the other. He had in a most unfair attempt to win the contest, ordered his mad scientists to make bombs and rockets that could fly all the way to Buckingham Palace. There were V2's (V1's too I think), buzz bombs, incendiary bombs and doodlebugs. Fired from across the Channel they flew over the White Cliffs of Dover and the green and pleasant farmlands and villages of Kent, up over the North Downs and straight past the marvellous but doubtfully effective barrage balloons; huge bunches of silver sausages sped straight at England's heart. Seeing for the first time nice close rows of houses (and getting a bit short of steam anyway) they dropped suddenly from the sky ten miles short of central London, slap bang onto Pickhurst Mead, Hayes, Bromley.

This didn't worry Hitler but it worried my mum and dad and several hundred thousand other mums and dads who were unfortunate enough to live along this extra dangerous line of fire. A German flying bomb down your chimney at two in the morning was considered an unwelcome intrusion into family life by all but the most eccentric and speedy evacuation was called for. Families tried to arrange temporary accommodation elsewhere if they could. My mother, brother Tony and me (soon to be born) were despatched to Hook Norton, a little village at the Eastern end of the Cotswold Hills in Oxfordshire. Hookey it was known as and as I say the word in my head and write it down, I can smell the burnt toast with paraffin and see a huge cold stone kitchen. Outside are sunny cottage gardens and deep flowered hedgerows where we gathered rose hips for the Vitamin C war effort. These images are accompanied by simultaneous feelings of a vague insecurity but also a curious comfortable cosiness.

Hook Norton was (still is) a beautiful place 20 or so crow miles North West of Oxford on the way to Banbury Cross. Several dozen yellow grey stone cottages, many pancaked thickly with grey thatch; others roofed with great slices of stone, a very solid old church and a justly famous little brewery. All this jumbled up between neatly folding farmers' hills, green, yellow, pale gold or stripey brown according to season. Our particular retreat was organised by kind family friends with connections in Hookey and a safer and more tranquil haven it would have been hard to imagine.

Tony, who must have been just over two (together with mother) were settled in with a friendly, capable lady, a nurse or midwife by trade who must have eyed my mother with professional glee. Given the

107

choice, I would very much like to have been born in her nice neat little cottage but I was not given the choice and in the event neither was my mother. Our lady lacked an indoor lavatory and various other facilities which were deemed requisite for my early days and we were moved by higher authorities to the nearby Rectory. This was a gloomy tower of a place with a gloomy tower of a Rector, both distinctly out of proportion with the surrounding cottages and parishioners.

My birth was in the nearby market town of Chipping Norton (Chippy) in a very sensible fully equipped square stone hospital, specially designed for the purpose. I was safely delivered, I am reliably informed, on the 27th of February 1941. A few days later we were on our way back along the winding lanes and over the hills to Hookey and The Rectory.

Life in this place, surrounded by so many willing, attentive and knowledgeable female hands, with the war so far away, should have been quite pleasant for a mother with two small boys, but we had the Rector to cope with. My mum soon discovered that she had escaped the wrath of one fearsome tyrant only to move into the very headquarters of another. He bitterly resented the intrusion of these evacuees, thoroughly disapproved of children in general and babies in particular, but reserved his special hatred for Methodists. Thus, with my mother being nominally a Methodist, I was a triple-headed devil. He was able to express this in a practical way by informing her that he had 'no intention' of christening her little heathen in his church.

This devout man was seven or eight feet tall and wore a great black dusty cassock night and day. The location of his waist was encircled by several yards of thick white whiskery string and the whole towering edifice was surmounted by a thick white whiskery head.

His daily routine began early out in the cobbled yard where he savagely worked the pump to raise the supply of water for his unwelcomely large household. While carrying out this task he could repeat his special curses of the day in time with the jerking of the handle. This completed, he turned his attention to a small flock of milking goats. I pray he was kinder to them than to the rest of us, but fear not.

Goat's milk was considered by 'modern mums' in those days to be a definite step backwards, a wartime expedient, a 'make-do' sort of substitute food. We realise now that it was good stuff and many of us war babies (including my wife Wendy, I discovered later) thrived on its wonderful properties. Think for a moment of the enormous contribution made to Art, Music, Theatre and Literature by this nation's citizens currently aged between 45 and 50 something years. I guarantee you'll find a diet of wartime goat's milk went down their little gizzards during their formative years.

His milking completed he carried it in a bucket into the great cold stone kitchen. Here he was now free to persecute and harass any babies, toddlers, mummies or dogs who were foolish or unlucky enough to cross his dark path. Just what had led such a person to enter the service of God must remain an eternal mystery. If The Almighty Himself did have an answer he was not letting on, maybe He was as confused as the rest of us. Such a man did not bring God, the Church or even religion into disrepute, he was quite simply nothing to do with it all.

While his temper waxed, Hitler's fortunes must have waned because we returned home for a while to inspect massive holes in the road and to hear of sundry damage and disasters both national and local. "A whole family in their bungalow up by the Common went just like that, poor souls". My father's youngest brother Colin had been captured on the other side of the world. He was a lovely uncle I was never to meet. Nearly every family had their own special grief. Soon the sirens were wailing again and we stumbled out in our dressing gowns to the damp, death-like, smelly Anderson shelter. It was built mostly of brick and concrete and was cramped inside. They were to provide ugly but useful garden sheds for many peacetime years. Huddled around a miserable candle we waited to be killed – "you won't even know its happened", or for the 'all clear' to sound. The 'all clear' was a different sound from the 'warning' and came as a great relief, no doubt, to grown ups. For me all tunes held the same mournful dread when played on that particular instrument of war. I hate sirens, even now.

It must have sounded too frequently again – was I about 2 years old? This time we went to Delabole in North Cornwall. This is a small village with a gigantic quarry, then supplier of splendid roofs to half the West Country. Wild and windy though it was we were tucked nicely under the sturdy slates of kind Mr. and Mrs. Pooley in their little miner's cottage. One rather less windy day, we set off on a great trek to see the sea along many Cornish miles (these are longer than our usual ones). We went down deep wild fuschia lanes to Trebarwith to eat Pooley pasties and to marvel at the vast sweep of golden sands and the enormous blue ocean for the first and most memorable time in my life. Back in the cottage kitchen our feelings of well-being had considerable spice added to them by the knowledge that there were a couple of dozen sticks of dynamite in the dresser next to the blazing Cornish range! Sensible Mr. Pooley, in common with his workmates, had borrowed the stuff from the quarry just in case. "Let thim Germins come roun' 'ere, We'll soon show 'em eh?" and they would have too.

Then we moved up country to ancient Wiltshire with its rolling hills strewn with stone age wonders to a dawdling ribbon of cottages, a fine church and a few farms, called Compton Bassett. Its great attraction for us was its proximity to my dad's current RAF station which was just a short bike ride along the lane.

I recall another long walk, this time to market day in sausage-famous Calne. This was something of a Marco Polo effort for my mother with two boys and the pushchair; she never being a great walker. Whether we had any aunts and grannies for porterage I don't remember. I do remember (can 'feel') the sweaty cold stone floor of the kitchen painted a violent blood red. It was so uneven that a toy car or ball couldn't possibly run true, a most unsatisfactory state of affairs for small boys. Soon, back home to Kent, presumably during another lull in the proceedings, we caught up on the latest tragedies and the dreadful price of things in the shops, "If only you could get them, mind." Living as we had been in our remote rural farming communities, we'd been a bit spoilt for vital commodities. Back in the suburbs with ration books and regulations, things weren't so easy to come by. Then it was that I must have begun to meet my neighbours for the first time. These were those boys and girls who were later to begin school with me and to be my companions, sweethearts and enemies for the next eight or nine years. I learned how to fall off my brother's Tri-ang trike and then to be brave enough to visit the stinky pig bins at the end of our road, but not the tank traps. The pig bins were where public-spirited householders were required to deposit items suitable to be boiled up for a wartime porker's diet. There wasn't much food about to create such dainty scraps but something must certainly have gone in there for them to smell as bad as they did. The tank traps were frighteningly deep ditches hurriedly carved across the corn and cabbage fields between us and Bromley, a couple of miles away. They were full of mud, newts and old prams and they would surely prove an insuperable obstacle to even the most cunning German tank commander. These were considered, next to Hitler himself, the most dangerous and unpleasant objects in the whole world and were to be avoided by all but the most foolhardy. Some years after the war, before they were filled in, my brother obtained an old motor cycle side-car built in the style of a small motor boat. No doubt it had been the height of fashion in its day twenty years before. Stripped of its one wheel it floated perfectly in the tank trap for several seconds, then disappointingly, gurgled under the surface, disappearing for ever in the bright orange sludge. None of its gallant crew were lost, I'm pleased to say, or you might not be reading this.

Tony and I also found time to have whooping cough. We did this neatly cooped up in the indoor 'Morrison' air raid shelter positioned where, in more normal times you might expect to find the dining table. The shelter had four mighty upright corner pieces, rigid steelmesh sides and a very thick bomb proof steel plate roof. All bolted firmly together they made remarkably sturdy chicken houses throughout the following decade. Our shared whooping cough was apparently very mild, unlike my chicken pox some time later. This was a truly marvellous manifestation of the disease. Womenfolk came from far and wide to see for themselves the wonder of it all. I was a star turn for a time and have some small scars to prove it. Hitler must have heard about my fame and his jealousy knowing no bounds, he recommenced his aggressions. We were suddenly returned back to Hook Norton and another dose of the dreaded Rector.

I was three then but Tony being two and a half years older was deemed ready for school. He was obliged to sit all day with half a dozen other luckless little souls on a long bench at a table that completely filled the front parlour of a cottage near the church. I suppose there must have been a teacher of some kind too to squash in. Just once (perhaps mother had gone to Oxford for the day) I was allowed to share this nigh-on adult ritual and was miserably forced onto the end of the bench. With hindsight, anything was better than spending it in the presence of the Rector, with only a dozen goats and grannies for protection. Later, I went to Oxford for the day and I think we went into a tea shop for half a bun. For some reason I thought I'd been to New York and it took several years to convince me otherwise.

One fine day I broke my leg. We were being hunted and chased amongst the beech trees of the Rector's garden by his sporting sons on their huge bikes. I dashed across the cobbled yard towards the relative safety of the kitchen but missed my footing on the step, Boo hoo hoo!

"He's broken his leg", said my poor mother, "perhaps he should go to hospital". "Don't be such a damn fool woman", said his holiness. "Make the boy stand, he's just being babyish again". I lay all night trying to prove my distraught mother's point. I remember my howling brought an enquiring mouse from beneath the skirting board and I could not run away. Eventually it warmed the dear Rector's heart, for sometime later (the very next day) he allowed the village doctor to inspect the offending limb. So off I went to the Chipping Norton hospital by taxi to receive a great thick white dollop of bandages and plaster. Other children were to become curiously envious and it gained much adult sympathy from all but the most heartless (no names).

I was too small for crutches apparently and spent happy days in the pushchair again, with much kindly female attention. I might well have received the memorable orange at this time for being such a brave little chap. Several weeks later, back in the hospital, they informed us that it was high time I lost my lovely new appendage. I remember with utmost horror the huge steel-cold bone shattering shears being slipped inside the grubby plaster. To my amazement I lived, my tears dried and I quickly learned to walk and run again (soon we didn't even remember which leg it was). My hour as a wartime hero was evidently over. So was the war itself grinding to a conclusion. Old Hitler had his back to the wall by now, our glorious Spitfires and the poor brave men who flew and died in them had given their all. We had clever old Winston Churchill with his big cigar and lots of strange

American soldiers with funny voices and chewing gum to bolster our confidence. Above all we were British. We were winning now and national pride was returning fast. Why had we ever been foolish enough to doubt our position as the greatest nation in the World?

We had been back home in Kent for some time though before victory was finally 'declared'. Spirits soon revived for some but there were also the bereaved. There were widows and orphans and my own dear grandfather who had lost his wife at the beginning of the war and his youngest son at the end. Gradually though, most of the men came home. Proud or shy in uniforms or 'demob' suits, full of strange and mixed emotions to greet their children, some for the first time. My wife Wendy was two years old when she and her dad first met.

Recovery from war was not instantaneous and there was little more in the way of fresh food in the Home and Colonial at the Station Approach, Hayes. What was available, whether by ration book or on the black market, was gathered together on one splendid occasion for our own street celebrations. Each end of Pickhurst Mead was blocked off to traffic (not that there was a lot of it about then), our bomb craters were carefully filled in and some trestle tables (normally reserved only for important flower shows) were set up down the centre of the road. This was our semi-detached neighbourhood Victory Party – we even had flags and blancmanges. Each lucky child was presented with a white 'Bakelite' beaker upon which was painted their own name, in thick orange paint, often spelt correctly. Surely it had all been worth it just for this? The orange squash flowed like water (which it was) and we even had jelly in different colours (but not flavours). It was a great fish paste sandwich day and one which I would not have missed for all the paint boxes in Woolworths. After the junketing there were the fireworks. It seems an odd way to celebrate the end of the bombing with even more bangs, fire and brimstone but we didn't worry about it at the time, for peace had arrived. And all too soon so had real school. There came a new predictable normality without the crushing explosions in the night and hurried departures. Soon to soften the blow, a few sweets and even some real bananas appeared. ''Don't eat those sweets all at once, you'll be sick'' was the warning. Try as we might there were never enough in the bag to really test the theory. We knew just what to expect when the first bananas arrived for there had been huge bunches of them hanging 'Waltons Fruit and Veg' right through the war. The difference was that you could eat these bananas (the others being but plaster and yellow paint – "just for show"). The "real ones" had to be mashed up with a small spoonful of granulated sugar; this precaution to prevent gastric disorders of an unspecified nature.

By the time I started school at George Lane Primary, I was already a serious artist and eager to be recognised as such. My Granny Spencer referred to my works as scribblings. Though I realised no unkindness was intended, I found it professionally offensive. My father, even though he had been in the RAF for five years, could not draw a Spitfire well enough to satisfy me and had to be corrected. I soon regularly supplied paintings for the walls of the school hall, no subject was really too difficult. Galleons in full sail were a speciality.

As an artist now I realise that those enforced times of evacuation spent in remote villages out in the true English Countryside where turnip and rose, cabbage and sunflower grew side by side in their beautiful orderly disorder, planted in me a love of such places that is lifelong. In my work nowadays I seem constantly to draw from a well of half-remembered and even instinctive images. Second only to my happy marriage and family life, this early experience of village doings has, I believe, been the strongest single influence on my work. It was mostly gathered before the age of three and a bit.

A year or two ago, with a couple of hours to spare between meetings with my publishers in Oxford, I returned to Hook Norton for the first time in nearly forty-five years. To my delight it was indeed the beautiful place of my childhood memories. These had played surprisingly few tricks on the scale, geography or the very spirit and atmosphere of the place over the years. I wandered happily about, half knowing what I was about to see around the next corner. Something made me decide that The Rectory would now be re-named, for it was unlikely that such a place was suited to the present day incumbent of such a humble parish. Just where I expected to find it, there was the too tall, gaunt stone house with great trees around it and the cobbled yard. Sure enough, set in the wall close by the gate was not 'The Rectory' nameplate but 'The Old Rectory', just as I imagined. So, I thought no Rector there now, nor any goats as far as I could see.

Earlier this year I was browsing through Brewers Dictionary of Phrase and Fable, a standard work I'm told for literary persons, academics and such. It is a treasure box too for ordinary mortals. The personal gem I found is reproduced below. I present it to you with considerable pride; strong memories of a certain tall man in black who probably was not really as horrid as I thought then and with grudging gratitude to old Adolf Hitler who certainly was.

Hog wild. In American parlance to go berserk (*see* BERSERK.)

Hog's Back. The western end of the North Downs, the chalk ridge from Guildford to Farnham in Surrey; so called from outline.

Hogs-Norton. A village in Oxfordshire, now called Hook Norton. The name owes its more recent fame to Gillie Potter, the English comedian and broadcaster, who described in mock erudite fashion a long series of unlikely events taking place in this village. **I think you were born at Hogs-Norton.** A reproof to an ill-mannered person.

> I think thou wast born at Hoggs-Norton where piggs play upon the organs.
> HOWELL.: *English Proverbs.*

Hoogen Mogen. Holland or the Netherlands, so called from *Hooge en Mogen* — high and

'Ill-mannered person' I may be. Perhaps the Rector did 'play upon the organs' but I never actually called him a 'pigg'.

Graham Clarke grew up not only to achieve fame as an artist but as an author as well. He is married with four children and lives in the village of Boughton Monchelsea near Maidstone, Kent's county town.

Faint Recollection
by
JOHN TALBOT

IT'S ONLY a faint recollection now, like a vague flickering image that leaves a huge gap in the detail. Sometimes a mostly forgotten trace reappears from some hidden recess in this imperfect memory. When that may happen can't be predicted. Why this mite and not that morsel return is a great mystery. Perhaps some childishly important point tagged the event and it remained whilst other, now more interesting relics, have vanished. Anyway, what the weather was like, and how I said goodbye, they are gone. What is still there today are memories of the haversack, the gas mask in its cardboard box, a lot of other children of my age, the teachers and the train.

Before that day there are other memories that matter in the telling of it. I can still hear Chamberlain's voice. Or is it that the message he conveyed in his broadcast has been repeated so many times that I believe falsely that I recall the original? I'm sure about the preparations for war and how absurd they seem now. Paper, wetted

117

in some way, stuffed in the cracks – 'to stop the gas coming in', the criss cross of brown sticky paper on the windows to stop flying glass when the bombs went off (not so absurd that one). The false alarms from the siren which were to become so familiar; the men enlisting, the uniforms, they're all firmly fixed as if they were background items which help to focus attention where it should be. Only it can't always be made to focus no matter how hard I try. And then the trivia, why does white chocolate bought from Arthur Nicholls' corner shop stick in the mind as it did on the hands? Why do I remember the lead toy soldiers, mother's curling tongs and Monday washing done in the copper? Another world it seems. And it was.

The train journey took a very long time, just how long I don't know. It was a special train managing to take us from Dover to the Welsh valley without needing to change en route. On the way, there was more evidence of mobilisation as we were shunted into sidings to give way to military equipment and troop trains. There was lots of schoolboy banter with much shouting out of windows whenever we managed to avoid the close scrutiny of the teachers. I seem to recall refreshments being dispensed by ladies from some volunteer organisation, sandwiches and tea or lemonade. It was all an adventure that is, until the boredom or the uncertainty set in.

It was dark when we arrived. The next thing I remember is the school hall in which we were gathered as if in some sort of market, to be 'sold' to the highest bidders. "Any two brothers? Two girl friends?". When allocated they disappeared with some strange person to who knows where? Well into the proceedings there was a call for two boys and Teddy and I shot our hands in the air not wanting to be left unsold, nor to be hived off alone in this foreign place. By now, as I recall, it must have been about two o'clock in the morning and we were half awake so that anything seemed better than staying wide-eyed in that uninviting room. I know now that the home we were to taken into was friendly, secure and warm, but then? Despite the tiredness it was no easy matter to go to sleep and morning came with a start. Teddy was sitting up cold and miserable. Days later, it was time to write home. Paper and pen were provided. It would take a different home and indifferent family for a kid in such a circumstance not be homesick. Dear Mum, I wrote, I'm not happy here, can I come home? But by the time I might have expected a reply I had found new friends, a new environment and all was right with the world. I got no reply. I was an adult before I discovered that the letter had been intercepted by a wise and canny 'aunty'. It had never reached its destination to cause anxiety to my mum. Now it seems that that kind of wisdom would be penalized by 'authority' rather than rewarded. Such is the change in a modern world grown used to discouraging such unilateral good sense.

I had found myself in a very special place and time. This was Welsh mining country with the closeness of community life and the fervour of its commitment to God, singing, the working-class and family. It provided a mixture perhaps unique in history and would all too soon disappear. I didn't know all this of course, not that is as a grown up, paid up, member of it would. But as a child, I feel it, smell it and even taste it too. I still do to this day. The memories are of the slag heap and the coal dust in the alley, the bracken and the whinberries on the mountain, the smell of baked scones for Sunday tea, and chapel. Oh yes, chapel above all. Sardis congregational. We went en masse and sang all the hymns with me singing as loud as any. The sermons were a different matter. The way I see them now reminds me of something someone once said about going to the opera as a social duty. It starts at eight and after its been going for what seems a couple of hours you look at your watch to find it's ten past eight. Well, I used to lean forward and gnaw at the varnished wooden pew in front of me to relieve the boredom and I can still taste that varnish today. What would bring me up sharp was the visit of a particularly fervent circuit preacher. He would start in a modest tone and gradually work up to fever pitch changing to 'the Welsh' and finally break into song until there was no one able to ignore him, not even me. It was heady stuff leaving its permanent mark like the armourer's stamp on a gun which identifies its pedigree. At the age we evacuees were at, we were like untempered steel, malleable, pliant, open to influence.

It was a sound experience growing up there. There was something of my boyish role model in it. I was Tom Sawyer and I could identify Huck. This 'Huckleberry Finn' came from Alexandra Road, where the outcasts lived. Quite what was so disturbingly different about "the outcasts" I can't say but we were certainly better than them! Even when a community is that close-knit and working-class, there is still a caste system at work. I had to be Tom, because, as a special treat

119

at the workman's hall and sitting on the hard seats, (the fourp'nees') I had seen the film. To add to the illusion there was my hour of fame when I fought Edgar Weinbaum. Edgar and I had some sort of minor dispute which it seemed impinged on our individual honour. However, we neither of us were quite prepared for what came next. Some of the offshift miners looking for some free entertainment no doubt, in a place which offered precious little, decided to take us in hand. So a boyish scrap became the world light-weight championship with timed rounds, corners, seconds and betting! It would have been more appropriate for Edgar and I to have posed a little, snarled a little, shaped up and gone our separate ways. We couldn't now of course, our cowardice would be exposed to the community. So we went several rounds, drew a little blood, mainly from knuckles and noses and enjoyed a moment of temporary fame.

At 'home', aunty had already become our "Mam". What a towering image she projects, even now, in my mind. An earth mother if ever there was one. "We don't have failures here, our Jack went to university." Getting on at school was not simply encouraged, it was demanded. And we all did get on. There was not one in that house that didn't 'win the scholarship'. It was in such circumstances that, after what seemed a lifetime but in reality could only have been a couple of years, I had to leave and find a home elsewhere. The grammar school children were evacuated to a different place. It was harder leaving my adopted home than it had been leaving Kent and catching that train from home with my haversack and gas mask. It was an episode of indelible quality which had passed into experience, leaving the fading memories which undoubtedly shaped the man I was to become.

The transfer to the grammar school in another part of South Wales took place in entirely different circumstances. I was older and a little wiser but then so were they. The patriotic fervour that led to people taking us in had grown a bit stale. It was compulsory billeting now and it all happened in the cold light of day. The system had the force of law and so it was implemented in that way. A sergeant of police, with evacuee in hand, arrived at the allocated address to pronounce the sentence.

"I've got an evacuee for you."

An astounded look appeared on the face of the reluctant new hostess who replied, "We don't want one here, we've got no room."

"You've got to have him" was the reply, at which stage I was thrust unceremoniously in through the front door and left with my new, rather aggrieved supervisor, with whom I was at least as unhappy as she was with me.

A limit was set on the time that the unfortunate billeting family had to put up with the intruder. Each new term brought another new experience. There was the old maid and her spinster daughter, then the apostolics who were forever proclaiming the second coming and so on. Not all the people were bad, of course, but none lived up to that first and happy home in the Welsh valleys to which I have returned. It will always be a part of my life that I would readily live again.

Despite being that much older, this second phase evacuation brings memories just as vague. Oddly it's much more the happy times that are readily recalled. Nothing you see, seemed to be lasting or forever; tomorrow was another day. Soon that other day arrived and the time had come for this passive invasion to end. I remember the ceremony in which we had rehearsed the song for our departure, 'Land of our Fathers' only to be swamped by sound when our hosts took up our lead and sang it in their native tongue. It was impressive, mind-boggling and spine-tingling.

It seems now to have symbolised that uneasy relationship, that clash of cultures. More than forty years on, the influence might be hard to detect in me, but whenever certain attitudes, deeply ingrained, collide with those of others which are too distinct to remember – it is then that I know it's there that something happened during my evacuee years. It is a certainty that needs no clearer picture. That faint recollection is for me enough.

Footnote

John Talbot was evacuated in 1940 with Barton Road Elementary School, Dover to Ynysddu in Monmouthshire. His hosts were the Schull family who still live there. Betty Schull married Jim Dowm and they live in the very house mentioned in the story. They also act as caretakers at Sardis which still survives though with difficulty. Sardis was built in 1906 as a Welsh chapel and for many years services were conducted entirely in Welsh. Later only the singing of hymns retained the language. Sardis is badly in need of repair but still provides a place of worship and one in which some interesting old photographs of early preachers can be seen. It is the sort of heritage which is without pretension and so easily overlooked.

Ynysddu is proud to be the birthplace of the poet Islywn who is buried just down the road at the little chapel of Babbath in Cwmfelinfach. The railway line that brought the evacuees is closed and it now provides a pretty country walk.

Edgar Weinbaum was an evacuee from Islington in London who came with a second wave after the Dover school.

Dover Grammar School were evacuated to Ebbw Vale and were presented when they left with a cup for rugby to be called the Ebbw Vale cup, which must still be in the school trophy room, though in all the years of evacuation they only managed one draw and lost all the other matches played against the local Welsh sides. To be fair they were and still are a soccer school.

John remembers very little animosity between the local boys and the evacuees but not a lot of mixing either, understandable perhaps when whole schools were transported as an entity.

John's eldest daughter lives in Dover and the Schull family became his relatives when, during the war, his uncle, the late and sorely missed George Boyson married Vashti Schull who lives right next door to her sister Betty.

John Talbot now lives in Bristol where he works for GEC Avionics. He is a widower and has four grown up children.

Through the Eyes of a Child

EVACUATION WAS a journey into the unknown. Strange places, strange people and often strange customs. For those children whose future destination was in the hands of the authorities, there was no way of them knowing what to expect. Many were very young. With the benefit of hindsight, they were probably too young to be sent away. Their memories in some cases are incomplete. They were simply too young to retain all of it.

Many people did not feel they had sufficient to offer to make a major contribution to the book. But they were more than ready to share their living memories. These "snapshots" complete the stories of those Children in Retreat.

MARY SWIFT OF SUNDRIDGE REMEMBERS HOW SAD SHE WAS WHEN SHE LEFT HER MOTHER AND HER HEADMISTRESS. . .

"My sister Kitty and I were the only two children to leave Brasted that day. Eventually we were put on the train with hundreds of other children, all labelled, and carrying cases or brown paper parcels. Some were carrying dolls and teddy bears, and we all had our Mickey Mouse Gas Masks.

It seemed a long journey. We ended up in Sidmouth, Devon. We were taken to a large hall, where lots of adults were walking around. All the children were ushered into the middle of the hall, and the adults walked around us. It was just like a cattle market. They only picked the child they liked the look of.

Eventually, Kitty and I were picked out by two elderly ladies. We went to their home by taxi. It was in the country. But when we arrived, the authorities had already sent them two little girls. So they asked the taxi driver to take us back to the hall. We were tired and frightened by this time. On the way back, the taxi driver took a short cut – through a large housing estate. He obviously knew the area, for he stopped his taxi to talk to a lady he knew. She was intrigued as to why he had two small girls in his taxi. He related the story to her. She felt sorry for us, and took us in for the night. That night turned into a day, into weeks, and eventually, to a much longer period. We had a really good time with Mr. and Mrs. Wood and their son, Terry.

There were so many things different from home. This included the food. Clotted Devonshire cream was new to us. Kitty liked it, I did not. Tripe and onions and mackerel were also new foods to us then.

I did not like the cream, so Kitty used to eat mine too. Small wonder that when eventually we went home, our parents did not recognise her. She had put on so much weight!

The family were into dramatics. While we were there, they were putting on a show. It was an Ivor Novello musical. I remember the song, "We'll gather Lilacs". The costumes – everything – was very authentic. On the evening, we were treated royally, and given the best seats.

Some of these snatches seem like yesterday. I think Kitty and I were lucky to stay with such nice people.

After the war, we went to visit them again, and were treated like family. That was the last I saw of all of them. Auntie and Uncle died within a short space of time. We do not know what happened to their son, Terry. But there is always the hope that we will meet up with him again".

FOR JOHN HOPPERTON OF GRAVESEND, HIS EVACUATION STARTED OUT HAPPILY, BUT SOON DETERIORATED. . .

"Myself and my three brothers were evacuated to Norfolk, on the Medway Queen. It was nice there and a lovely man and lady met us at Cromer. Initially we all slept in the church hall on straw sacks. But in December, after three months in Norfolk, we had to leave for Cheadle, Staffordshire.

We really suffered there. Both at school, and the house we stayed in, the three 'S's' were more in evidence than the three 'R's'. These were, Strap, Stick and Slipper. The second day there it all started. I had kicked a tennis ball with a local lad. He (not I) kicked the ball into the headmaster's garden. I was blamed for this misdemeanour, not him. To add insult to (eventual) injury, I had to get the stick from the headmaster's study. It came from the cupboard covered in cobwebs. He said it was the first time he had used it in four years. He laid it on hard, twice on each hand. I was only seven years old.

My brothers and I found everybody was "strap" happy wherever we went. It was almost as though they wanted to punish us for going there.

We were shoved around, and from the Midlands to Scotland, all seemed strap-happy. There was a particular man and lady who we stayed with who were brutal. The strap was 4″ wide, with a brass buckle. We had had a three hour journey. For dinner, they gave us six chips and an egg. Oliver Twist-like, I asked for more. The lady replied, "More of my husband's strap, or slipper, more like".

In the school, in Cheadle they wrote. . ."Why don't you go home you Southern Pigs?". We wanted to, but there was no way of getting there.

We had gone in 1939. Eventually, we returned home in July 1942. My dad had been a prisoner of war. When he came home he weighed just 6st. 4lb., and had contracted tuberculosis. By comparison, I suppose we were lucky. But we still bear the scars.

My brother goes back, periodically. He cannot forget that nearly every day he was strapped by the headmaster. In 1979, he saw an article in a daily newspaper about a school in Blackpool where evacuees had been sent. The placard said. . ."DON'T STRAP ME SIR". My brother was convinced that the headmaster of that school was the same one we had had in Cheadle. Time passes, but you never forget".

MRS VIOLET ARTHUR FROM WIGSTON, LEICESTER HAS REASON TO THANK HER EVACUATION. THROUGH IT, SHE MET HER HUSBAND...

"I was evacuated when war broke out in 1939, from Deal with the pupils from St. Mary's Roman Catholic School. We were sent to Tondu, Aberkenfig, South Wales.

Before our walk to the railway station at Deal, everyone was given a medical examination, allotted a tag to be tied on our lapels, stating whether or not we were suffering from any form of illness, or had head lice. After tearful farewells, we were on our way. The train stopped at one station throughout the journey. Here, we saw soldiers on their return from Dunkirk. Most of them were tired and weary after their ordeal, but they still had time to make friends with the evacuees, or to give us their tea and biscuits. These had been provided -for them by various organisations.

We arrived at Bridgend, where again we were given a medical examination, and then put into groups to go on to various places. We arrived at Tondu at 5.30 pm and were taken to the local school.

While waiting to enter the school, we were spat upon by the local children. Eventually we entered the school to find local dignitaries there – the Mayor and Postmaster – to name but two. They were sitting at a long table. After looking down their lists and selecting the children who they thought paired off well, we were then sent to the families who had applied to take us. By 11.30 pm, there were four children left – myself included. Twenty minutes later I, with another small girl of nine years were left. Nobody seemed to know what to do. Following debate, the girl (Doris) and I were taken to a house a couple of streets away. The house we came to was in darkness. After loud knocking, a bedroom window opened. A head appeared. The "head" asked what we wanted. Our escort explained our situation – "These are your evacuees Mrs. Thomas". The "head" replied, "Take them back, I don't want them". We were taken back to the centre. There, panic set-in. Nobody knew what to do. It was the postmaster who said, "Hubert Mead and his wife will give them a bed for the night".

This time by car, we were taken to another house. On opening the door, Mr. and Mrs. Mead said that they had been told that no more evacuees were available. Seeing how tired and exhausted we were, Mrs. Mead took us in. She gave us supper and gave us a bed. All this was done on the promise that we would leave again the following morning. We stayed for fourteen (very happy) months.

After returning home, I began to write to Mrs. Mead's nephew who was serving with the Royal Air Force in India. After his demob a few years later, we met, courted and married in 1954. I like to think that had it not been for my evacuation, I may never have met my husband".

MR. B.G. GRAY OF ORPINGTON HEARD THE APPEAL FOR STORIES ON A LOCAL RADIO STATION, RADIO KENT. HE COMMENTED THAT IT BROUGHT BACK MEMORIES OF A LONG TIME AGO. . .

"I was evacuated to Leicestershire. I was then ten years old and my sister was five. Although we had stayed at home during the Battle of Britain, we were sent away when the flying bombs started. My mother did not want us to go, as she would be left on her own.

Dad was then a prisoner of war. She insisted at the time, that we went together. I felt strongly that I wanted to go away – all my friends were going.

(Editor's italics. . ."What follows is a sad comment of war, but probably a true reflection of the hopelessness that people felt at that time. . .")

"My mother said she had had her life, and I could go if I wanted. As I grew up, I realised how cruel my remarks must have seemed to my mother. At that time, she was only in her thirties. But with the determination of youth and the devotion of a parent who put my needs before her own; she relented and I got my way.

We lived in Bromley at that time. We met at the school (which was fairly typical, I imagine). I cannot remember about food. We got onto a coach, with all the mums waving goodbye. They took us to Bromley South Station, and then onto Victoria. When we arrived, we were greeted by a buzz bomb. We were told to dive for cover. Consequently, after the "raid", although we had left home clean, we were filthy from our "dive" onto the platform. I remember my sister crying, because she thought Mum would tell her off for getting her coat dirty.

Somehow we arrived at Marylebone Station, (I have no idea how). Eventually, we arrived in Loughborough. From there, to the village hall in Lileby. There, we slept on the floor. But here, a lady who had been helping out at the reception centre took my sister and I to her home. She said we had angelic faces. This as events turned out, was probably our downfall.

The lady was upper-class and middle-aged. She had no children of her own. Her husband owned his own business, and they were unused to the ways of children. They had a lovely home. Every time we went indoors we were told to take off our shoes. That went against the grain.

She used to hit us with a dog whip, for all sorts of minor misdemeanours. I honestly do not think we were that bad. When I teased and tormented my sister – which is normal sibling behaviour – the lady used to get the Billeting Officer to come to see us.

We went to the local school, but were taught by teachers from the Bromley area. As I was a choir boy in the local church choir in Bromley, I became a member of the local church choir.

We had been away for four months when my mother came to see us. I was too young, and have no idea what was said, but shortly after the visit, we returned home. We came home with dirty and verminous heads (so much for the upper classes). My sister never forgave Mum for burning her hat! We also came home to face the rockets (or V2s)''.

MRS. PATRICIA WALLER OF HOO, CANNOT FACE, EVEN NOW THE THOUGHT OF RETURNING TO THE SCENE OF HER EVACUATION...

''I was about seven when I was evacuated. I cannot remember the year. I do not remember too many details, except how awful it was. We were living at Folkestone at the time, but my father was at Dunkirk.

I think probably due to the heavy bombing, my mother was convinced we were all going to die. I was scared, and can remember begging my mother to send me away. Other children were to be evacuated. I was so scared.

We were evacuated to Wales, in Pontnewydd, Newport. When we arrived, all the old ladies in the village (who were superstitious) thought that as this was co-incident to air raids on Wales, we had brought bad luck in with us. When we arrived, all the old ladies lined the village streets and were spitting at us.

Another recollection was that the village pond was full of dead cats and dogs. When the bombing started, people apparently just drowned their animals and left them in the pond, rather than taking them home to give them a decent burial. They should have been killed more humanely.

We were taught locally by a teacher from our school. But unfortunately, she got sick, and had to return home. From then on, we had lessons in Welsh. Their value was questionable. None of us understood the language. Apart from occupying our time, it was a pointless exercise.

I contracted impetigo and felt dreadfully ill. I had no stamp, nor the money for it, but I wrote to my mother, and put the letter into a letter box. My mother received this and came and collected us, and brought us home. It was an awful experience. Even now, I cannot visit Wales. The memories are too awful''.

A BAD ENOUGH EXPERIENCE FOR MRS. WALLER, BUT HER MEMORIES DO NOT END IN WALES...

''Because of the problems of living near to the coast, we eventually moved to the Medway Towns. But here, we were again subjected to some traumatic times. Again, we all became frightened about the future. Other children were going away, this time, to Gloucester. Again, we were to be very badly treated. The woman with whom we were billeted took our clothes and food coupons. This was normal. But the woman then, instead of using these for our benefit, sold the coupons on the black market.

My brother and I were made to sleep on the floor. It was dreadful. The woman was a real ''con'' artist. She would go around to the Vicar's wife and plead our case. ''I have these evacuee children etc.'' The result was that the Vicar's wife gave her her old clothes, which we then had to wear. We were a very sorry sight. We were wearing adult clothes, rather shabby, which totally swamped us.

We were like tramps, and by this time, rather flea-ridden too. Because the mattress on the floor was damp, my brother became ill. He had contracted tuberculosis. Again, in sheer desperation, I sent an un-stamped letter to my mother. She came, saw, and collected us. Later, she admitted, she was ashamed of us when she saw us. My mother recalled how, at Swindon Station, she made us stand away from her further down the platform, so that people did not realise we were together.

Upon our return home, my brother was terribly ill. He almost died. Both of us had to have our hair cut-off because it was so flea-ridden and tangled. My mother reported the woman to the authorities. I have no idea whether anything was done about it".

RADIO KENT ALSO PROVIDED THE LINK FOR PAUL MILES OF EAST MALLING TO RELATE HIS REMINISCENCES. . .

"I was born in January 1939, and did not even realise that the family I was living with were not my own family. Only in 1946, when I was the last of three brothers and one sister to be re-united with our father and step-mother, did I realise that things for me had been different.

The family home was in Kentish Town, North London. I never knew my natural mother, who had apparently died from blood poisoning. I can only assume that at this time, my father was a serving soldier, because when the family were re-united, I learnt that Peter, my eldest brother had stayed in London with my grandmother. All the other children were sent to different places.

As a baby (or small child) I don't really know which, I went to Cuxton, to a foster family. This was to a house called "Dolce Royden" at White Hart Hill. They had children of their own, but I do not remember the two eldest who were boys. I do however, remember the youngest daughter, Kathleen. I have vivid memories of those years.

I can remember being at school when a doodle bug came down nearby and the explosion broke all the windows.

My foster parent, Mr. Foster, kept chickens, which was fairly normal then. I was asked to take some eggs to someone in the village. Going downhill on a three-wheeled bike, I hit the gas lamp-post half way down and broke the eggs. I do not remember the actual form of chastisement, but do remember the reference to "a clumsy Londoner".

I can also remember a soldier visiting me, and giving me a matchstick firing gun. I learnt later that this was my father. I can also remember the soldiers visiting the area ready to embark somewhere, and with my toy gun proudly displayed at them, was told "Don't shoot".

I can also remember the flying boats being tested on the nearby River Medway. An even better kept secret was the testing of the submarines in the yards at Wouldham, which was nearby. I never saw one!

Metal shelters with wire sides in the bedroom, pieces of shrapnel, wireless accumulators and paper criss-crossed windows can all be remembered, but I did not know why. There was no deprivation or shortages that I recall. But, as a five year old boy by then, I thought it all normal.

Suffering their own war were my father and step-mother. In October 1946 a lady, my step-mother, arrived at Cuxton and took me to a new home. On arrival, I found I had two brothers and a sister.

I did revisit the Fosters in 1952, but have never been back since. I pass the house occasionally, but the name plate "Dolce Royden" is no longer there.

Although in adulthood, I have often thought about the strange logic which sent me from London to Kent, fifty years on I can only be grateful both to the organisation which arranged it and offer thanks to those people who took me in".

Conclusion

A people at war is, in itself, an evocative phrase. Children at war is simply an alarming concept. But this is what this book has been about. At the end of a long task, one is sometimes relieved, sometimes disappointed that the journey has reached its climax. At the end of this particular task, there is a feeling of sadness, not for the (then) children – all of whom showed remarkable resilience. Sadness that the authorities forcibly imposed war on the lives of children, not in a sharing sense with their parents, but in a totally alien environment. Today society would not tolerate it, but in 1939 attitudes were different. But there was one household which seemed to have the right idea. It is an example of a family, who felt that their children should share the dangers and privations of the British people. The quote comes from Queen Elizabeth (now the Queen Mother) in response to the suggestion that Princess Elizabeth and Princess Margaret should join the exodus of the children. . ."The children can't go without me," said the Queen firmly. "I can't leave the King, and of course the King won't go".

Joy Richardson
July 1990

Acknowledgements

TO PRODUCE a book of this kind needs contributions from many sources. Throughout my research, so many people have been helpful and kind. Letters from people simply to give me encouragement have done just that.

Others have made a more significant contribution, and so thanks are owed to:-

> The Mayor of Dover
>
> The Mayor of Gravesend
>
> Arthur Percival of the Fleur de Lis Heritage Centre in Faversham
>
> Terry Sutton, Dover Express Newspaper
>
> The Kent Messenger Group of Newspapers
>
> Adscene
>
> The Gravesend Reporter Newspaper and most of the other local newspapers in Kent
>
> Christine Anderson of Kent County Council Public Relations
>
> Tricia Rowsby and the Staff of Kent Archives Office
>
> The Kent County Council – for providing us with Libraries and local studies centres
>
> BBC Radio Kent – for putting me in touch with so many wonderful people who gave me the flavour for this book

And by no means least, Allison and Susannah Wainman of SAWD PUBLICATIONS who gave me endless help and encouragement to see the task through.

Finally to John, my long-suffering husband for this sterling efforts as chief cook and bottle-washer and endless patience in letting me use him as an audience for the work.